YORK NO

General Editors: Profe
of Stirling) & Professo...
University of Beirut)

E.M. Forster

A PASSAGE TO INDIA

Notes by Vasant A. Shahane

PH D (LEEDS) *Professor of English*
Osmania University, Hyderabad

LONGMAN
YORK PRESS

Extracts from *A Passage to India* by E. M. Forster are reprinted
by kind permission of Edward Arnold Ltd., London; and in the
USA by kind permission of Harcourt Brace Jovanovich, Inc.,
New York, copyright 1924 by Harcourt Brace Jovanovich, Inc.,
renewed 1952 by E. M. Forster.

YORK PRESS
Immeuble Esseily, Place Riad Solh, Beirut.

LONGMAN GROUP LIMITED
Longman House, Burnt Mill, Harlow,
Essex CM20 2JE, England
Associated companies, branches and representatives
throughout the world

© Librairie du Liban 1982

First published 1982
Thirteenth impression 1995

ISBN 0-582-03350-0

Produced by Longman Singapore Publishers Pte Ltd
Printed in Singapore

Contents

Part 1

Introduction

The life of E.M. Forster

Edward Morgan Forster was born in London on 1 January, 1879. His name, Edward Morgan, emerged out of a comic confusion recorded by Forster himself. In London the baby was registered as 'Henry Morgan Forster,' and later in March, he was taken to church at Clapham Common for christening. On the way the verger asked the baby's father what the name of the child would be, and he absent-mindedly gave his own name and therefore the baby was christened Edward Morgan. 'I had been registered in one way,' Forster writes, 'and christened another. What on earth was to happen! It turned out after agitated research that the christening had it, so Edward I am!'

Forster's recollections of his childhood are faithfully recorded in the biography of his great aunt, Marianne Thornton, which he wrote in 1956. Marianne called her favourite nephew the 'Important One'. The great aunt, who was in her eighties, began to write letters to Morgan Forster when he was only eighteen months old. This correspondence seemed extraordinary since Morgan at that time 'was probably crawling on the carpet'. He began to write to her later and the letters were exchanged in the same house which was known as Battersea Rise and was in north London; she wrote to 'Morgan Forster, Esq., Upstairs.' The 'Important One' was left a legacy of £8,000 by his great aunt, which not merely facilitated Forster's education at Cambridge, but also helped him to travel to Italy and Greece, and eventually made his 'career as a writer possible'.

Forster was educated at a preparatory school in Eastbourne (1890–2) and as a day-boy at Tonbridge School (1893–7). His school life was unhappy and restrictive; he entered King's College, Cambridge in 1897 and was soon charmed by the openness, freedom and intellectual atmosphere of the university. Forster was a great lover of houses and places such as Rooksrest, a later family house (he later called it 'Howards End' in the novel of the same title), and King's College, of which he was made an Honorary Fellow in 1945. He then resided in his rooms at King's almost till his death in 1970. In his will, he left all his earnings and estate to the college. Forster reacted adversely to the working of the public school system with its emphasis on collective action, its regimentation and implied disregard for the value of personal relations. Cambridge, on the other hand, seemed to him to stress these very qualities, the charm of personal relationships and free intellectual intercourse, which stemmed from its liberal and humane traditions. It was at King's that Forster formed his life-long friendships with many persons who later became famous. He obtained his Classical and Historical Tripos from King's in 1901. Cambridge became a major source of his creative imagination, as was shown in his novels *The Longest Journey* (1907) and *Maurice* (1971). He writes nostalgically about his ideal, selective Cambridge: 'O spare Cambridge! Is not the city a little one? Is she not unparalleled?'*

Forster is a rare and special man. He is rare because he is in part a late Victorian and an Edwardian and in part a modern. Forster's life, then, extends over a very long period (1879 to 1970) marked by rapid social and cultural changes. Yet it is his aesthetic response that makes him a very rare and special writer. Humanism, liberalism, intellectualism, freedom and an acute sensitivity—such are the qualities of the temper of the twentieth century to which Forster has given his allegiance as man and writer.

A Passage to India

Forster's *A Passage to India* has been recognised as a major work of British fiction. Published in June 1924, it is Forster's fifth novel, and probably his greatest. His sixth novel, *Maurice* (1971), was not published until after his death. With the publication of *A Passage to India*, Forster achieved international recognition, and critics and commentators in England and America readily acknowledged the artistic talent he displayed in this classic presentation of a liberal point of view.

However, contemporary critical responses to *A Passage to India* were somewhat mixed. Soon after its publication, L.P. Hartley, a sensitive critic, discovered the novel's cosmic significance. '*A Passage to India*', he wrote, 'is much more than a study of racial contrasts and disabilities. It is intensely personal and (if the phrase may be pardoned) intensely cosmic.'† Virginia Woolf praised it as a novel marching triumphantly and sadly 'through the real life and politics of India, the intricacy of personal relations, the story itself, the muddle and mystery of life'.‡ Contemporary approaches emphasised the elements of social realism and Indo-English relations in *A Passage to India*. Forster's portrayal

*E.M. Forster, *Two cheers for Democracy*, Edward Arnold, London, 1951, p.357.
†L.P. Hartley, review of *A Passage to India, Spectator*, 28 June 1924, pp.1048–50.
‡Virginia Woolf, review of *A Passage to India, Nation and Athenaeum*, 24 June 1924, p.234.

of Anglo-Indians caused annoyance to the British bureaucracy in India, and one civil servant, E.A. Horne, explained 'how the book strikes an Anglo-Indian—a task for which I claim to possess qualifications having spent the last fourteen years of my life in Chandrapore (Patna) itself.'* Horne thought that the Hindus and the Muslims in the novel were 'real enough', but that the Anglo-Indians were very 'unreal': 'What planet do they inhabit?' he asked, 'They are not even good caricatures.' This contemporary controversy in the British press reflected very mixed reactions to *A Passage to India*.

Even as late as 1954 Nirad C. Chaudhuri, an eminent Indian writer, wrote that *A Passage to India* is primarily a political novel with Indo-English racial overtones. He overemphasises its political aspect when he says that *A Passage to India* has possibly had an even greater influence on British imperial politics than on English literature.† It became a popular and powerful weapon in the hands of anti-imperialists in England and also in India. Liberal Englishmen, on their first voyage to India, made a point of reading it with a view to mapping out their own passage to this baffling country. On the other hand, Paul Scott, revaluing the novel, stated that those who saw themselves caricatured as Anglo-Indians 'threw copies overboard from the P. & O. [steamships of the Peninsular and Oriental line] into the Red Sea.'‡ Appreciative critics saw in it a passage to 'more than India,'§ whereas unfavourable commentators called it a 'passage to less than India.'

Ideas and beliefs

Forster is a creative artist, moralist, and thinker. These three roles are dexterously harmonised in his fictional art. As a thinker he is essentially the product of a liberal and humane culture emanating from an environment deeply influenced by the Evangelical creed, utilitarianism,¶

*E.A. Horne, *The New Statesman and Nation*, 23 August, 1924, p.568.
†Nirad C. Chaudhuri, 'Passage to and from India,' *Encounter*, June 1954, pp.19–24.
‡Paul Scott, 'How Well Have They Worn?' *The Times*, 6 January, 1966, p.15.
§Benita Parry, 'Passage to More Than India', included in *Forster: A Collection of Critical Essays*, ed. Malcolm Bradbury, 1966, p.164.
¶Utilitarianism is an ethical concept which holds that all human actions must be judged according to their utility in promoting the greatest happiness of the greatest number of people. This idea, enunciated by Jeremy Bentham, gained strength in England in the nineteenth century. The Clapham Sect was a group of very intelligent, wealthy and practical reformers who flourished between 1790 and 1835 in England. It may be described as a brotherhood of Christian social workers devoted to abolition of the slave trade abroad and improved measures of prison and other reforms at home. Bishop Wilberforce was its leader and Henry Thornton, Forster's grandfather, one of its leading members.

political liberalism, and the ideas propounded by the eminent people known as 'apostles'.* He was also deeply influenced by Greek and Roman literature and culture and the ideas and beliefs associated with the Greek view of life.

Forster came into close contact with the Cambridge Apostles and their intellectual milieu. The circle of his friends was wide and included Lytton Strachey, John Maynard Keynes, Desmond MacCarthy, Clive Bell, Leonard and Virginia Woolf, Vanessa Bell, and Duncan Grant. These people later came to be known as the Bloomsbury Group and claimed adherence to G.E. Moore's ethical concepts and Roger Fry's aesthetic ideas.†

Forster championed the cause of humanism and classicism, yet he remained in the mainstream of the nineteenth century romantic tradition. He himself was essentially a romanticist, a symbolist, almost a poet in prose fiction. Indeed he was a true inheritor of the traditions of the poets: Blake, Coleridge, Wordsworth and Shelley, traditions basically romantic; and he projected a synthesis, an alliance of intellect and intuition, reason and imagination, faith and scepticism.

The growth of the English novel is deeply linked with moral values and the parable form of Forster's early novels, *Where Angels Fear to Tread* (1905), and *The Longest Journey* (1907), demonstrates the moralist in him. Forster, however, was an informal moralist since he reflected the ethical ideas and beliefs of G.E. Moore who valued the enjoyment of personal relationships and the aesthetic appreciation of works of art.

The liberal idea

Though the central conception of liberalism is political, its literary and aesthetic context seem to govern Forster's mind and values. Liberalism politically implies a system of government in accordance with people's

*The Apostles were members of a secret discussion society organised at St John's College, Cambridge by George Tomlinson in 1820. It was also called 'the Society'. It later moved to Trinity College and King's College. Forster himself joined the Apostles in 1897.

†G.E. Moore was a well-known Cambridge philosopher whose book *Principia Ethica* (1903) presented, in his own words, 'a scientific Ethics.' He believed that the pleasures of human association and the enjoyment of beauty are valuable experiences. Forster valued friendships and also beautiful objects of art, and therefore his attitudes were similar to those of the Bloomsbury Group who were Moore's admirers. Roger Fry wrote *Vision and Design* (1920) and *Last Lectures* (1939). He wrote on aesthetics. Beauty and art are primary concerns of aesthetics.

will, and this view is linked with the English idea of human progress through the use of science and technology. The liberal idea is also allied with the concepts of tolerance, of dissent and individual freedom. Forster has a commitment to the liberal tradition of progress, freedom and humanitarianism. His novels, therefore, demonstrated the liberal idea in human and social relationships. His fiction was sensitively shaped by his liberal imagination. Yet Forster was not always in tune with this liberal tradition. He was primarily an individualist who believed in the individual citizen's freedom in a society left free from excessive governmental pressure or compulsive policies. Receptive to new ideas of social welfare, he believed that an ideal society must show a combination of new economy and old traditional morality. He was also deeply influenced by the creative aspect of liberalism which is related to the writing of fiction. This creative element in liberalism accepts both good and evil in its sphere.

Forster discovers and delineates liberalism in human relationships, in the coming together of different levels of classes, in middle-class English girls making liberal discoveries in the arms of Italian lovers such as Gino Carella in his novel *Where Angels Fear to Tread* (1905)—or seeking union in love with English boys belonging to a lower cultural stratum of English society such as George Emerson in his novel *A Room with a View* (1908). Forster's deep involvement in the processes of liberal imagination gives rise to the novel as social comedy, thereby forging a link between him and the tradition of the English novel shaped and nourished in the nineteenth century by Jane Austen, Charles Dickens and George Meredith. Forster's close association with the Bloomsbury Group is, of course, well known but he was also deeply influenced by persons and ideas outside this group, especially by the fiction of Marcel Proust and Henry James. James used the phrase 'international situation' to indicate the coming together of persons from different countries, specially Americans and Europeans. This resulted in an interaction of two cultures which provided a new subject matter for fiction. Forster's novels also are shaped by this international situation.

Forster's humanism

Forster was essentially a humanist who believed in education, culture and freedom. Humanism is a school of thought and beliefs which gives prime importance to man in his relationship with nature and society. Forster's ideas seem similar to those of Coleridge who subscribed to a romantic and organic view of life. Forster is a writer in the Coleridgean tradition, a humanist and symbolist.*

It must be stated that humanism and humanitarianism in the Victorian age were multifaceted movements which cut across many divisions of social and political thought. They encompassed many diverse elements and beliefs. The literary heritage of humanism gives meaning and substance to Forster's creative work. It is also rooted in his family, the Thorntons, which added to it the authenticity of a personal experience.

Forster was thus a rare combination of creative writer, moralist and humanist. His fiction was marked by the sensitivity of a poet, the discriminating sense of a moralist and the deep concern for culture and freedom of a humanist. He was also a novelist of ideas.

A note on the text

A Passage to India was first published by Edward Arnold, London, 1924 and Harcourt Brace, New York, 1924. All page references in these notes are to the Uniform Edition of the novel, published by Edward Arnold, London, 1971.

The edition published by Dent in the Everyman Series, London, 1942, contains notes by Forster.

---

*A symbolist uses symbols as objects which represent something abstract as, for instance, a dove presented as a gesture or symbol of peace. Forster, in writing his novels, seems to move close to poetry. Liberalism and humanism are in this way related to his Romantic heritage and his poetical quality.

Part 2

Summaries
of A PASSAGE TO INDIA

A general summary

Chandrapore town is partly old and partly new, and except for the Marabar Caves it does not seem extraordinary in any way. Its old Indian part is somewhat unplanned whereas its British civil station is carefully planned and modern. In this town Aziz works as a doctor, an assistant to Major Callendar, in the Government Hospital. He has a close circle of friends: Hamidullah, a barrister; Mahmoud Ali, a lawyer; and others. They discuss Indo-English social and personal relations and the haughtiness of English women. Aziz is sent for by Major Callendar but on arrival finds that the Major has gone out. On his way back, Aziz enters a mosque where he meets an elderly Englishwoman, Mrs Moore. Aziz instinctively likes her and their conversation is extremely friendly. We learn that she is the mother of the City Magistrate, Ronny Heaslop. She is accompanied by a young girl, Adela Quested, who has arrived from England to explore the possibility of marrying Ronny.

Both Mrs Moore and Adela express their wish to see the real India, and Mr Turton, the Collector, arranges a 'Bridge Party' to enable them to meet Indians. This party is not much of a success because the English and the Indians do not get beyond surface civilities or casual conversation. However, they meet Cyril Fielding, the Principal of the local government college, who is a liberal and friendly towards Indians. He invites them to tea at his house where Mrs Moore and Adela meet Aziz and Professor Godbole. At Fielding's tea party, Aziz is in fine spirits. He talks to Adela of Mogul emperors and the glory of that age. He then invites them to visit the Marabar Caves and the ladies accept his invitation. They also talk about the Marabar Caves but Professor Godbole does not explain their significance to the visitors. Ronny Heaslop arrives to take the ladies to a polo match and the cordial atmosphere of the party is dramatically disturbed. Professor Godbole sings a song which describes the milkmaiden's love for Shri Krishna, and the tense atmosphere is greatly relieved.

The friendship between Aziz and Fielding grows steadily. Fielding visits Aziz to enquire about his health. They discuss Indo-British relations and also the problems of religious belief and unbelief. Aziz, in a rare gesture of friendship, shows Fielding his dead wife's picture.

Fielding is touched by this. Aziz tells Fielding that what India needs is kindness, kindness and more kindness. Fielding says that he will not marry, and that he is an agnostic. (An agnostic is one who neither believes nor disbelieves in God.) Fielding says he would rather leave a thought behind him than a child. He calls Adela priggish. She seems to him a pathetic product of Western education. She tries to understand India as if it is a part of a lecture. She is, of course, very sincere. Fielding believes in personal friendships, in individuals, in freedom. He speaks to Aziz, informally outlining his set of beliefs.

In Part II the Marabar Caves are described in detail. The Ganges, according to Hindu mythological beliefs, flows from the feet of Vishnu and Siva's hair. Vishnu and Siva are the names of Hindu gods who form, along with Brahma, the Hindu Trinity. The Marabar Hills are situated in north-east India; they contain the famous Marabar Caves which are older than all spirit. Nothing is inside them. One of them is called the Kawa Dol.

Aziz makes elaborate preparations for the Marabar expedition. He stays at the railway station. Mrs Moore and Adela arrive on time to catch the train. But Fielding and Godbole are delayed and left behind. Aziz and the others reach the caves. Mrs Moore enters the first cave; something strikes her and she is greatly affected. She asks Aziz and Adela to go ahead. She sits down as though she has had a physical breakdown. But she has lost her will to live, her desire for personal relations, even her religious beliefs. Everything seems to be reduced to nothingness—'boum'. She has a vision or a nightmare, and is totally changed by this experience.

Aziz and Adela move on to the other caves in the mountain range. Adela asks Aziz how many wives he has, and he is pained by this question. He moves into another cave to regain his balance, and finds that Adela has gone out of sight. He shouts for her, and slaps the guide, then finds Adela's broken field-glasses. He returns to the place where Mrs Moore is, and is pleased to see Fielding there.

While she is in the cave Adela realises that she doesn't love Ronny after all. She hears an echo, which is a symptom of her inner malady. She climbs down a hill and is pricked by cactuses. She returns to Chandrapore in Miss Derek's car. Fielding, who observes this, is surprised by Adela's unexpected action.

When the others return from the Marabar Caves to Chandrapore, Aziz is arrested on arrival at the station and taken to prison. Fielding is shocked. Aziz is said to have tried to molest Adela in the Caves and is arrested on a charge of attempted rape. The atmosphere in Chandrapore suddenly becomes tense. Mohurram also adds to the tension.

The trial of Aziz creates social and political tensions in Chandrapore. Aziz's friends make preparations for his defence in court and Mr Amritrao, a reputed lawyer, is engaged for the purpose. Fielding forsakes his countrymen, resigns from the Anglo-Indian Club, and openly supports Aziz. Adela, who is staying at the house of the Callendars, says she suffers from an echo. Mrs Moore loses her will to stay in India and decides to go back to England even before the trial. Fielding speaks with Godbole about Aziz and the Marabar episode only to find that the mystic is more involved in philosophical speculations than in the pressing, rigid realities of life. The trial creates distrust between Indian and English people.

At the trial of Aziz, Mr McBryde presents the case for the prosecution. He outlines all the relevant details. But answering the crucial question as to whether the prisoner followed her into the cave, Adela says that she is not quite sure. This most unexpected withdrawal of the charge destroys the case for prosecution. Mr Das, the magistrate, is left with no alternative but to dismiss the case and declare Aziz not guilty.

Adela renounces her own people, and her echo is silenced. Mrs Moore seems to her to have approved of her action. It is the moment of Aziz's triumph. The Anglo-Indians are shocked by this strange turn of events. Fielding escorts Adela to his house where she stays. He joins Aziz in his victory celebrations. Meanwhile the news of Mrs Moore's death on her voyage to England is made known. Aziz, who admired Mrs Moore greatly, is deeply pained. The engagement between Ronny and Adela is broken off. Fielding persuades Aziz to give up his claim for damages from Adela for wrongly implicating him in the case. Chandrapore officials are transferred and a new set of officials takes charge of the administration. Adela leaves Chandrapore for England—a sadder and a wiser woman. She decides to look up Ralph and Stella, the children of Mrs Moore's second marriage.

The scene now shifts from Chandrapore to Mau. Godbole is the Education Minister in this small native state. Aziz, disgusted with British India, has become the personal physician of the Maharajah. Fielding, too, has become an inspector of schools in this area.

Professor Godbole dances on a carpet before the images of the god. It is the time of the Gokul Ashtami festival (the festival of Lord Krishna's birth) which is celebrated with great merriment. People play practical jokes upon each other. Godbole is in a heated state, almost in a trance, in which he perceives Mrs Moore with the wasp. (She had earlier in the novel noticed a wasp on a hat-peg; it is a part of India, of the universe.) This is his mystic vision. He tries to achieve union with God and 'God is Love.' He loves Mrs Moore, the wasp, Aziz,

Fielding and everything else, animate as well as inanimate objects. He sings a song about Tukaram, an Indian saint. The theme of the song is man's unity with God. He invokes his personal god to 'come' and satisfy his innermost desire.

Godbole informs Aziz of Fielding's arrival at the Guest House. Fielding is on an official visit to the area for inspection of schools. His wife and her brother have also come to Mau. Aziz suspects that Fielding has married Adela and that he has been robbed of the compensation money. Fielding wishes to watch the torchlight procession near the Mau tank. A prisoner is released as an annual remembrance of the legend of the Shrine of the Head.

Aziz, along with his children, walks in the grounds near the shrine. The Rajah is dead, but the news is not released because it will mar the festivities and the procession. Aziz meets Fielding and Ralph. Ralph is pursued by the bees and a bee stings him. Aziz and Fielding talk, but their conversation is neither intimate nor friendly because of his suspicion that Fielding has married Adela, the primary agent of his suffering. However, he now learns that Fielding has married Stella, Mrs Moore's daughter. The misunderstanding is cleared up. Aziz visits the Guest House and gives Ralph, Mrs Moore's son, medicine for the pain caused by the bee sting. He learns that Fielding and Stella have gone out boating on the Mau tank. The boating scene is significant, because it removes all barriers and divisions among men. Aziz and Ralph also join the boating scene. Their boats collide and they fall into the shallow water only to realise the unity of all men. This is a triumph of India, of love, of harmony.

However, this unity is not everlasting. Aziz and Fielding go on their last horse-ride in the Mau jungles. Fielding wants Aziz to be friends with him again as in the past. However, Aziz says that they cannot become true friends unless India becomes a free country and all Englishmen as rulers leave India for good. Only on the basis of political equality is true friendship between two individuals possible. Fielding asks again, 'why can't we be friends now? ... it is what I want. It is what you want.' But the environment, the setting, natural and human, doesn't want it: 'No, not yet,' and the sky said, 'No, not there.'

Detailed summaries

Part I: MOSQUE

Chapter 1

The first chapter of 'Part I: Mosque' in *A Passage to India*, though very brief, is crucial to the structure of the novel since it outlines the physical features of Chandrapore as well as the principal themes of the novel. In less than three pages Forster sketches the outlines of Chandrapore town (which, in fact, is based on his knowledge of Bankipore, a cantonment town near Patna in Bihar) and the geography of the area appears almost a prelude to the geography of the mind. 'Edged rather than washed by the river Ganges,' Chandrapore 'trails for a couple of miles along the bank.' Its streets are 'mean' and its temples 'ineffective'. Though a few fine houses exist, Chandrapore is neither large nor beautiful, and there are no paintings or carvings in the bazaars. 'The very wood seems made of mud, the inhabitants of mud moving' and the town symbolises 'some low but indestructible form of life'.

There is a complete contrast between this Indian part of Chandrapore and the civil station designed and built by the British. 'The prospect alters,' says Forster, 'hence Chandrapore appears to be a totally different place.' It is a city of gardens, a 'tropical pleasance' washed by the Ganges. Systematically planned, it reflects the English sense of organisation and skilful construction. The roads intersect at right angles. This civil station 'shares nothing with the city except the overarching sky'.

Forster introduces two major symbols in this chapter: the sky 'which settles everything' and the Marabar Caves which are 'extraordinary'. 'The sky is a dome of blending tints,' though primarily it is blue or white. It stands for space and its immense vault seems to be lit at night with innumerable lamps. The sky can be a source of benediction because it is so enormous and strong, drawing its strength from the sun. The endless expanse of flat earth is interrupted by the fists and fingers of the extraordinary caves. The use of the word 'fists' suggests the aggressive or evil quality of the hostile rocks, the Marabar Hills, though it is difficult to pin down precisely their meaning or function in *A Passage to India*.

Chandrapore is indeed a miniature India of the nineteen-twenties—a country groping in the dark in search of her destiny, of diverse and divided people, an ancient land ruled by the British Government in India. Chandrapore town, with its Indian areas and its British Station complete with its exclusive club, highlights one of the principal themes, of division and union, fission and fusion, the Self and the Non-Self. *A Passage to India* is in some respects a political novel and the conflict of race relations, between English and Indians, and among Indians themselves, is foreshadowed in the physical features of Chandrapore town itself. The regional geography of Chandrapore in the first chapter, in this sense, appears to anticipate the divisions of social life and cultural conflicts.

NOTES AND GLOSSARY

maidan:	an open space or plain near a town
Eurasians:	people of mixed European and Asiatic parentage or descent
toddy palms:	trees yielding palm juice used as country liquor
neem trees:	margosa trees found in abundance in India. (botanical name: *Melia aradiracta*)
mangoes:	sweet, fleshy fruit of an Indian tree
pepul:	a large Indian tree with long leaves
tanks:	ponds, pools or reservoirs of water
civil station:	a refined part of the town which is not used by the army or military establishments

Chapter 2

This chapter treats Indo-English relations as a major theme. The Indians, Mahmoud Ali, Hamidullah and Aziz, are engaged in a serious and sad conversation—they were discussing 'as to whether or not it is possible to be friends with an Englishman' (p.8). Mahmoud Ali rules out the possibility of friendship; Hamidullah disagrees with him but with so many exceptions that their conclusions are almost the same. Hamidullah, the Western-educated lawyer, complains against the haughtiness of the 'red-nosed boy', Ronny Heaslop, the City Magistrate. Even Mr Turton, the bureaucratic District Collector, says Hamidullah, was once friendly and intimate with him, and had even shown him his stamp collection. The complaints of these Indian Muslims against the British officers in India are directed against their haughty behaviour, vanity, imperviousness to personal relations, and the overbearing superiority of the 'mem-sahibs' who seem even more offensive than their husbands. These Anglo-Indians (the term used in its nineteenth-century connotation, which includes Englishmen born or serving in India) display a blind arrogance towards Indian civilisation and do not believe in any real, personal or close social intercourse between the Indians and the British. Their view of Indo-English relations is purely official, even officious, and their task only a matter of administering a subject race in a wretched country. Any real attempt at social intimacy or forging personal relations is looked upon with grave doubt, if not with veiled contempt.

Mahmoud Ali and Hamidullah are, of course, not totally blind towards the kindnesses of a few Englishmen and Englishwomen, but they are bitterly critical of the general pattern of the behaviour of Anglo-Indians in contemporary India. Aziz is in no mood to discuss the pros and cons of the English officialdom in India: 'Why talk about the English? Brrrr . . .!' (p.10). He wishes to shut them out and drift into the garden. He gives evasive replies to Begum Hamidullah when she presses him to get married again since he is a widower with three children. After dinner, Aziz begins to recite scraps of poetry—Arabic, Persian and Urdu—dealing with his favourite themes, the brevity of love and the decay of Islam. The Indians, especially the Muslims, take a public view of poetry (unlike the English who take a private view of it). In this poetic scene, India seems 'one' to them and their own. They never care to analyse or interpret poetry but are rather carried away by mere words and high-sounding names. They show a pseudo-romantic taste in the appreciation of poetry.

This goodly dinner party at Hamidullah's is rather unexpectedly disturbed by a note from Major Callendar, the City Civil Surgeon, who is Aziz's boss at the hospital. Aziz is summoned to meet the Major at his bungalow, presumably to attend to a 'serious' case. His first reaction is not to clean his teeth, but he does this on the way to make himself more presentable to his boss. He rides a bicycle which is punctured on the way, and he has to get into a tonga (a horse carriage) to reach the place. The streets named after victorious British generals further deflate Aziz's ego and he approaches the bungalow on foot. But the Major is out and he hasn't left any message. Meanwhile, as if to add insult to injury, Mrs Callendar and Mrs Lesley take his tonga, and the servile assistant doctor in Aziz says courteously, 'You are most welcome, ladies' (p.15). This portrayal of Aziz, of a sentimental and cowardly man, is realistic and human.

After this unpleasant experience, Aziz wants 'to shake the dust of Anglo-India' off his feet! He is 'an athletic little man, daintily put together', but strong. On his way back he enters a Mosque near the European Club. The beauty and quiet atmosphere of the Mosque always please him and especially the ninety-nine attributes of God on the frieze give him great joy. His spirit is deeply stirred by the Mosque and he feels both spiritually and imaginatively involved in it. To him Islam seems 'more than a Faith, more than a battle-cry, more, much more . . .

Islam, an attitude towards life both exquisite and durable, where his body and soul found their home' (p.17).

Aziz greatly values the 'secret understanding of the heart' which is symbolised by the Mosque. He imagines that he will build a small mosque and a tomb which will carry a Persian inscription emphasising the value of the secret understanding of the heart! He feels as though he is in a dream watching the quivering pillars of the Mosque. Suddenly he sees an old Englishwoman and shouts 'Madam ... you should have taken off your shoes! ...' (p.18). Mrs Moore replies that she has already taken them off and Aziz begs her pardon. Her words, 'God is here,' touch him deeply. They sit for a while and talk about their families and children. Aziz is so deeply moved that he even confides in Mrs Moore his intense dislike of Major and Mrs Callendar. Mrs Moore tells him that she does not understand people, she only knows whether she likes or dislikes them. Aziz responds instinctively to her view: 'Then you are an Oriental,' he exclaims.

Mrs Moore and Aziz in the Mosque seem like two innocent, well-meaning, sincere and sentimental children of God. Their warm and close relationship is forged in this extremely delicate scene of their meeting in the Mosque which is indeed a genuine alliance of kindred spirits.

NOTES AND GLOSSARY

funeral of Queen Victoria: Queen Victoria (1819–1901) who became Queen in 1837

Cawnpore: (Kanpur) large industrial city in Uttar Pradesh in north India situated on the bank of the Ganges

champak: an Indian tree of the magnolia family, of great beauty, with scented flowers

Urdu: a language of the camp developed from Hindustani written in Arabic script

Hafiz: Khwaja Shamsuddin Mohd. Hafiz (1320–89), a well known Persian poet of Shiraz of the fourteenth century, who was a great composer of *ghazals* (lyrics)

Hali: Altaf Husain Hali (1837–1914), Urdu poet and critic; a strong advocate of reforms in Urdu literature and Muslim society

Iqbal: Sir Mohommed Iqbal (1875–1938), Urdu and Persian poet and philosopher; a great literary figure in Urdu literature. He was an advocate of a separate state for Indian Muslims (modern Pakistan)

chuprassi:	a peon or janitor or porter
'O Tonga wallah':	'O horse-carriage driver'
rupees:	the monetary unit or silver coin of India
Huzoor:	an honorific form of address, equivalent to 'Sir'
Punjab mail:	a fast train from Bombay to Delhi and the Punjab
Deccan:	literally the south of the Indian peninsula
Cousin Kate:	a popular play of the twenties
Civil Surgeon:	a government medical doctor, the chief of a district hospital

Chapter 3

In Chapter 3 Adela Quested expresses her inmost desire, 'to see the real India' (p.22). Mrs Moore has come to India, along with Miss Adela Quested, a 'queer cautious girl.' Adela wishes to observe Ronny Heaslop, Mrs Moore's son by her first husband, at work under a tropical sky and then to decide whether or not to marry him. She is almost bored by the performance of *Cousin Kate* at the English Club. She is delighted to know that Mrs Moore has strolled out of the Club, entered the Mosque and met an Indian. Mr Turton, with his good humour, tells her that Heaslop is a 'Sahib, ... he's the type we want, he's one of us' (p.23). Adela repeats her wish to see the 'real India,' which is scorned by Mrs Lesley and Mrs Callendar. However, Mr Turton, the Collector, offers to organise a 'Bridge Party'—'a party to bridge the gulf between East and West'—for Adela and Mrs Moore to meet the Aryan Brother, a gesture which is both genuine and amusing. On reaching home, Ronny learns that Aziz has been talking to Mrs Moore about Major Callendar and he wishes to pass on these remarks to his colleague. Mrs Moore is almost scandalised by Ronny's attitude, his rejection of the sanctity and secrecy of personal relations. Later, he promises not to let the Major know about Aziz's comments, and in return he asks his mother not to talk to Adela about Aziz and the complicated problems of Indo-English relations.

As Mrs Moore hangs up her cloak, she observes a small wasp on the peg. The wasp is an ambivalent moral symbol, of good-and-evil, since it is pretty but it may also sting. She exclaims to the wasp, 'Pretty dear' (p.33).

NOTES AND GLOSSARY

mem-sahibs:	ladies or wives of civil or military British officers
Collector:	the name for a chief revenue officer of a district in British India

lingo:	slang for 'language'
National Anthem:	'God Save the King'
Jehovah:	(Yahweh), the Hebrew God, a name used by Christians
Native State:	Indian State ruled by Indian maharajahs during the British rule in India
pukka:	(*Hindi*) strong, thorough, solid, complete
Burra sahib:	a Hindi word meaning a boss or important officer
Vakil:	a lawyer or an attorney practising law
trap:	a light, two-wheeled carriage
Benares:	the holy city of the Hindus situated on the Ganges river in Uttar Pradesh
MP:	Member of Parliament
izzat:	a Hindi word meaning reputation or respectability

Chapter 4

In this chapter Forster narrates at length the meeting of East and West at the Bridge Party arranged by the Collector, Mr Turton. Invitations have been issued to various individuals, but even these are looked upon with suspicion by Mahmoud Ali, though others welcome and appreciate Turton's intentions. The Nawab Bahadur, a benevolent landlord and philanthropist, responds enthusiastically. The missionaries, who believe that 'invitations must proceed from heaven perhaps' (p.35), are not on Turton's list of guests.

NOTES AND GLOSSARY

Nawab:	a Muslim prince or noble; a title bestowed by the British government

Chapter 5

The Bridge Party itself is not what Mrs Moore and Adela have expected it to be, partly because the Anglo-Indian ladies, especially Mrs Turton, behave rather stiffly. Mrs Turton, the Collector's wife, exclaims awkwardly to Mr Turton, 'What do you want me to do? Oh, these purdah women! I never thought any would come. Oh dear!' (p.39). Forster is conscious of the rather uncertain quality of the status of Indian women, some of whom turn their faces away from their hosts at this party. Their male relations stand separately in the grounds of the garden demonstrating the compartmentalised life of Indian men and women in the twenties. Mrs Turton detests the idea of even shaking hands with any of them; she only condescends to shake hands with the Nawab Bahadur. She also speaks a few words of welcome in Urdu, most of it in the imperative mood.

While Mrs Turton behaves stiffly and awkwardly, Fielding, Adela and Mrs Moore make amends for this odd behaviour. Mrs Moore begins to converse with the Indian ladies, a few of whom speak English. As an educated Indian lady mentions 'Eastbourne, Piccadilly, High Park Corner' (she means Hyde Park Corner in London), Adela beams with joy at the opportunity for conversation. These women have visited Britain and Mrs Turton is worried that they may apply Western standards to her conduct. She is told that they have visited Paris. 'They pass Paris on the way, no doubt,' said Mrs Turton, as if 'she was describing the movements of migratory birds' (p.40). Forster satirises Mrs Turton brilliantly, and the effect is partly comic, and partly ironic.

Forster's satire is directed with equal ingenuity against the Indians as well, especially the Bhattacharyas. Mrs Moore and Miss Quested desire to call on Mrs Bhattacharya and want to make an appointment: 'When?' she asks, and says that all days and timings are convenient. 'Thursday . . .?' 'Most certainly' is the positive reply. Mrs Bhattacharya's gesture 'implied that she had known, since Thursdays began, that English ladies would come to see her on one of them, and so always stayed in' (p.41). The celebrated Indian confusion which baffles a punctilious Westerner is skilfully satirised. The Bhattacharyas promise to send a carriage to fetch Mrs Moore and Adela, but it never turns up.

Mr Turton conducts himself well at the party, trying to be hospitable and pleasant. Mr Cyril Fielding, the Principal of the College, is very cordial, and moves freely among the Indians; Mr McBryde too behaves politely. The efforts of other Englishmen are frustrated by their women-folk, who spoil the party. The Bridge Party does not really get beyond an exchange of surface graces and superficial civilities, and Adela's desire to see the real India remains unfulfilled. However, the Bridge Party leads to Mr Fielding's invitation to Mrs Moore and Adela to come to tea at his house on Thursday.

Ronny and his mother, Mrs Moore, talk about India and Adela's reactions to the country and her people. While Ronny presents the common-sense bureaucratic point of view, Mrs Moore looks at India as part of the Mother Earth, part of the benign cosmos. She says, ' . . . India is part of the earth. And God has put us on the earth in order to be pleasant to each other. God . . . is . . . love' (p.50). While Mrs Moore tries to take a religious view of the world, Ronny adopts a secular world-view in which Englishmen seem to pose as gods.

Aryan: Indo-Germanic or Indo-European in origin. Now generally used for Indians speaking these languages

Pathan: person belonging to the North-West Frontier Province of India, now in Pakistan

Quality Street: a play written in 1902 by James Barrie (1860–1937)

Yeomen: gentlemen serving in a royal household or small estate-holders

Parsi: a descendant of the Zoroastrians (of an ancient religion founded by Zarathustra) who emigrated from Persia to India in the eighth century

Eastbourne: a seaside resort in Sussex in England

Piccadilly: a famous street in London

Hyde Park Corner: one of the busiest traffic centres in London

gram: chick-pea; pulse generally

dogcart: a two-wheeled horse vehicle with seats back to back

bhang: an intoxicant (made from leaves of hemp)

P. & O.: Peninsular and Oriental Steam Navigation Company, which operated regular steamer services between Bombay and London

Julienne soup: a soup made of vegetables cut in thin strips

Maharani: the Queen

pack her off to the Hills: send her (Adela) to hill stations in summer

Alpha and Omega: the beginning and the end (the first and last letters of the Greek alphabet)

Chapter 6

This chapter explores the relationship between Aziz and Major Callendar. Forster's portrayal of Aziz shows the assistant surgeon as a simpleton, a sentimental person, a man of mercurial temper, almost a bundle of contradictory traits. By profession, Aziz is a surgeon but 'it was his hand, not his mind, that was scientific' (p.51). For a while he behaves like a medical practitioner, and at other times like a pseudo-romantic poetaster. He has no genuine taste in poetry as he is pretending, or falsely seeming to be, a romantic. He and his boss have had many rows between them, and the latest one concerns his failure to report when summoned. Aziz, of course, tells him the truth, that his bicycle was punctured in front of the Cow Hospital, but the Major, without realising that Aziz had gone to Hamidullah's place, misunderstands him and walks away in a fit of anger. Aziz almost ignores the Major's moods and even feels that 'the English are a comic institution'.

Aziz does not attend the Bridge Party mainly because that day happens to be the anniversary of his wife's death. Although he has earlier agreed to attend the party with Dr Panna Lal, he decides to go to the Post Office. When the time for it approaches, he begins to remember his married life; how at first he disliked his wife, and later began loving her for her sincerity, affection and devotion. She had died in giving birth to his second son. He takes out her picture and his eyes fill with tears. He decides never to marry again but to continue to cherish the memory of the dead. He goes to Hamidullah's again. Hamidullah has gone to the party but his pony has not, and therefore Aziz takes it out for a ride. On his return home, he finds a letter with an official stamp. It is Fielding's invitation to him to come to tea.

NOTES AND GLOSSARY
chukker: round
Brahminy Bull: a zebu or a humped domestic ox

Chapter 7

Cyril Fielding has arrived in India rather late in life; he is over forty and hard-bitten when he boards his first Indian train at Bombay. He is sweet-tempered, easygoing, friendly, affectionate and extremely informal. His career is scholarly and varied; he has visited many countries and, in consequence, has developed a broad outlook. He believes principally in two basic values, of education and culture. He has been appointed Principal of the Government College at Chandrapore.

Fielding and his fellow-countrymen in India do not see eye to eye on many issues of personal relations, cultural and racial attitudes. On his first train journey he had met two Englishmen; one, a very young man fresh from England and the other a sun-dried Anglo-Indian, and he soon discovered that a gulf divided them. His liberal outlook and his desire to be friendly with Indians created a barrier between him and the official, rather officious, Anglo-India. He subscribes to the 'give-and-take of private conversation':

> The world, he believed, is a globe of men who are trying to reach one another and can best do so by the help of good will plus culture and intelligence—a creed ill suited to Chandrapore, but he had come out too late to lose it. He had no racial feeling—not because he was superior to his brother civilians, but because he had matured in a different atmosphere, where the herd-instinct does not flourish. (p.60)

Fielding does not of course believe in the theory of the 'white man's burden' nor in the 'superiority of the white race.' He is unaware that 'white' has as little to do with a man's complexion as God has to do with 'God Save the King'. He is both an anti-imperialist and, in a way, an agnostic. Good-natured and amiable that he is, Fielding believes that it is possible to be friends with both Indians and Englishmen, but it is impossible to cultivate these relationships if Anglo-Indian women are involved. Anglo-Indian women consider themselves 'very superior' to the Indians and their haughtiness and insolence work as a grave barrier to any possibilities of friendship and cordiality between the English and the Indians in the social and political situation of the nineteen-twenties. Fielding is not very eager to receive ladies at his college; he has, however, invited Mrs Moore and Adela because they are newcomers and have not been spoiled by the Anglo-Indian women's tribal ethic.

Fielding lives in a beautiful house in an ancient garden in the large grounds of the college. He is dressing in his bedroom when Dr Aziz is announced. Fielding shouts from his room to Aziz 'Please make yourself at home' (p.61). These five words hold the key to their initial relationship. Fielding is very informal and unconventional and this aspect of his behaviour appeals to Aziz immensely. It appears that Aziz has already heard about Fielding and, in fact, wishes that he would fall ill some day so that they might meet. They start on a gay note when Fielding suddenly stamps on his collar stud. Aziz immediately offers him his own gold collar stud and this incident, though small in itself, is suggestive of Aziz's instinctive liking for Fielding and also his generous nature:

'You know me by sight, then'
'Of course, of course. You know me?'
'I know you very well by name.'
'I have been here such a short time, and always in the bazaar. No wonder you have never seen me, and I wonder you know my name. I say, Mr Fielding?'
'Yes?'
'Guess what I look like before you come out. That will be a kind of game.'
'You're five feet nine inches high,' said Fielding, surmising this much through the ground glass of the bedroom door.
'Jolly good. What next? Have I not a venerable white beard?'
'Blast!'
'Anything wrong?'
'I've stamped on my last collar stud.'
'Take mine, take mine.'   (p.62)

Aziz is not merely impressed by Fielding's unconventional behaviour but also by his untidiness. He is delighted to know that he has been invited to meet two English ladies, Mrs Moore and Miss Adela Quested, and he suddenly recalls the romance of the meeting in the mosque. Aziz is told that Miss Quested is artistic, and he casually speaks of Post-Impressionist art (Virginia Woolf, one of Forster's friends, opened a controversial exhibition of Post-Impressionist paintings in London in 1909), a comment which rather baffles Fielding. Aziz at first misunderstands Fielding as one who seems to scoff at the 'obscure' Indian's attempt to look as civilised as the English ruling class. However, Fielding's fundamental goodness melts the thin ice of these superficial suspicions and Aziz begins to respond with affection. Aziz is more sensitive than sensible—he is indeed a dreamer. Fielding implies that Post-Impressionism, rather than the Indian, is 'obscure' and the air is cleared.

Mrs Moore and Adela arrive and Aziz feels deeply drawn to them. Adela refers to Mrs Moore's meeting with Aziz in the mosque and says that it helped the elderly lady to understand India. They discuss the Bhattacharyas' lapse in not acting on their invitation and their offer to send a carriage to fetch Mrs Moore.

Their conversation then turns to an interesting issue, which has a significant bearing on the novel's theme and structure: is India a mystery or a muddle?

'I do so hate mysteries,' Adela announced.

'We English do.'

'I dislike them not because I'm English, but from my own personal point of view,' she corrected.

'I like mysteries but I rather dislike muddles,' said Mrs Moore.

'A mystery is a muddle.'

'Oh, do you think so, Mr Fielding?'

'A mystery is only a high-sounding term for a muddle. No advantage in stirring it up, in either case. Aziz and I know well that India's a muddle.'

'India's—Oh, what an alarming idea!' (p.67)

Forster's use of the two words 'mystery' and 'muddle' is central to the novel's total meaning and also his own attitude to India. Is India a muddle or mystery? Perhaps it is both, or perhaps it is neither. An answer to these questions will depend upon the reader's attitude towards the final implications of the novel.

Aziz invites Mrs Moore and Adela to visit him and they accept this invitation, which proceeds directly from Fielding's tea and the Bhattacharyas' fiasco. Aziz is both irrational and emotional when he talks about the Mogul Emperor's love of water and fountains. He is certainly wrong about the water gravitating uphill into the tank. Ronny would have pointed out his mistake; Adela uncritically accepts his statements as true. Fielding now cares chiefly for truth of mood rather than verbal truth, and says nothing.

Meanwhile Professor Godbole arrives and the talk turns to Indian mangoes. Adela says that the effort to 'make India in England' or 'England in India' is frightfully expensive and even 'nasty.' Since Adela has taken Aziz's invitation seriously, he thinks of another place for the party, as his own house is unclean and awful. He cries 'I invite you all to see me in the Marabar Caves' (p.72).

Adela and Mrs Moore ask them about the Caves in the Marabar Hills, about which Aziz has some knowledge, although when Professor Godbole tries to describe the Caves to the guests he cannot really say anything positive. Adela cannot grasp the undercurrents of the dialogue about the Marabar, nor does she realise that a simpleton like Aziz 'was encountering Ancient Night' (p.74).

Ronny suddenly drops into this curious conversational game, a bundle of dilemmas. He asks Adela to accompany him to the polo game, and ignores both Aziz and Godbole. He is very officious with the two Indians, and Aziz, too, is provocative. He is in the air, flying on imaginary wings, and he will not come down to earth without a struggle. It is a tense, dramatic situation. Ronny tells Fielding that Adela should not have been left 'smoking' with two Indians, one of whom (Aziz) is 'a bounder'. In this tense atmosphere the formal leave-taking begins and the people seem either cross or wretched:

> 'Could one have been so petty on a Scotch moor or an Italian alp?' Fielding wondered afterwards. (p.76)

A long series of good-byes ensues, indicating only surface politeness and a somewhat tense atmosphere. Aziz shakes hands with Adela, reminds her of the invitation to the Caves, and rather tactlessly blurts out, 'What a shame you leave India so soon! Oh, do reconsider your decision, do stay' (p.77). He is perhaps unaware of the implications of this remark and its impact on the relationship between Ronny and Adela.

In this rather strained atmosphere, Miss Quested says to Professor Godbole, 'It's a shame we never heard you sing' (p.77). Professor Godbole responds positively and begins singing a song. His voice seems to have rhythm, and also melody. It is a bird's song; only the servants understand it. Fielding asks Godbole about the theme and he replies that it is a religious song. He imagines himself as a milkmaiden (Gopi) who prays before the Lord (Krishna), 'Come! Come to me only.' The god refuses to respond. Then he makes another humbler request to the god. 'Do not come to me only. Multiply yourself into a hundred Krishnas, and let one go to each of my hundred companions, but one, O Lord of the Universe, come to me ... He neglects to come' (p.78).

Godbole's song symbolising the god's refusal 'to come' anticipates the novel's slow but sure movement towards a godless universe—the Marabar Caves. Ronny's walking away in the middle of the haunting melody is the first sign of the fissures that are seriously to affect the world of human relationships in *A Passage to India*.

NOTES AND GLOSSARY

purdah:	veil used by Muslim women; also the curtain by which they are screened from strangers, and hence this system of seclusion
Mogul Empire:	a Mohammedan-Tartar Empire in India, founded by Babur (1483–1530) in 1526. It almost ended with the death of Aurangzebe (1707)
Peacock Throne:	the famous jewel-studded throne of Shah Jehan, the Mogul Emperor. It was carried to Iran by Nadirshah
Post Impressionist:	Post-Impressionism is the art of a more 'advanced' style than Impressionism, in which representation of form is subordinated to the subjective view of the artist
Loggia de' Lanzi:	a public square or piazza, consisting of three gigantic arches dominating one side of the main square of Florence
Maude Goodman:	a minor painter, here his paintings are referred to
dhoti:	a fabric used for loincloths by Indian men; the loincloth itself
Rains:	the rainy season in India—from June to September
Elephanta:	beautiful caves of Siva and Parvati near Bombay
Siva:	a god of the Hindu triad also known as Mahadev
Parvati:	Hindu goddess, wife of Siva

Chapter 8

In this chapter several events are narrated to unfold the aftermath of Fielding's tea party and Godbole's song. Forster traces the growth of human relationships, especially the mutual responses between Adela and Ronny. Adela was painfully surprised by Ronny's behaviour at Fielding's party. She promptly opens fire on him as soon as they begin their drive home and Aziz's invitation is discussed:

'Out where?' asked Ronny.
'The Marabar Caves.'
'Well, I'm blessed,' he murmured after a pause. 'Did he descend to any details?'
'He did not. If you had spoken to him, we could have arranged them.'
He shook his head laughing.   (p.79)

The insensitivity of Ronny's attitude to Indians, especially towards Aziz, is brought home to Adela in several ways. Ronny ridicules Aziz's shabbiness, saying 'there you have the Indian all over: inattention to detail; the fundamental slackness that reveals the race' (p.80). Ironically, Ronny's criticism of Aziz's dress, the collar climbing up his neck, has been a result of his lending the stud to Fielding, a sign of his generosity. Mrs Moore, who is rather annoyed, refuses to see the polo. Adela and Ronny go to the polo ground. She says she wants to have a 'thorough talk' with him and declares that she has decided not to get married to him. Although the news is hurtful, Ronny takes it in his stride and this shows a decent side of his character. She wants to clarify, to explain, and to understand Ronny's reaction too. Like two cool-headed English persons, they merely agree to part, and remain friends.

They meet the Nawab Bahadur and he offers to show them round in his car. On their way, their car runs over an animal and skids. Neither Ronny nor Adela is upset by this accident. The car has been hit by a hyena and they try to follow its footprints. However, Miss Derek arrives and they get a lift to Chandrapore in her car. On reaching home, Adela caresses Ronny's hand and says she would like to take back what she has said on the polo ground. The event of the hyena touching the car creates physical contact and feelings of love between Ronny and Adela, who normally are not emotionally involved. Mrs Moore says she wants to go back to England. She also expresses her affection for Aziz. On being told of the small accident caused by the hyena on the Marabar Road, she suddenly exclaims 'A ghost!' (p.95). Adela and Mrs Moore begin to play a game of patience. The old lady cannot explain why she uttered the words 'A ghost!' It is a coincidence that the Nawab Bahadur also speaks about the same event with his admirers. He recalls that he had run over a man on that road many years ago, and believes that the man 'continued to wait' there to attack him—it is so mysterious! It is a 'racial secret' which could be communicated only through blood, not through speech. Surprisingly, Mrs Moore's instinctive reaction to this event is similar to the Nawab's, and both views are shrouded in mystery.

NOTES AND GLOSSARY

crammer's:	an establishment offering special tuition
Charing Cross:	name of a railway station in London (also the area or locality) opened to traffic in 1864
topi:	hat or cap
Ruling Race:	here, the Anglo-Saxon or British race
Maharanis:	queens or ladies of royalty
Ranis and Begums:	queens and ladies of nobles
geyser:	a slang term meaning 'silly old fellow'; usually spelt 'geezer'
Krishna:	Lord Krishna, the Hindu god
peon:	attendant

Chapter 9

Aziz has an attack of fever and is forced to lie in bed. His thoughts wander about pretty women in Calcutta, but he checks this tendency to voluptuous imagining because he wants to remain 'respectable'. He ignores the Sunday church bells, which give a call to Anglo-India and also symbolise the missionary's endeavour. Aziz's friends, Hamidullah, Syed Mohammed, and Mr Haq call on him to enquire about his health. Quite surprisingly Professor Godbole, too, has been taken ill after Fielding's tea. Aziz feels sorry for Godbole's sickness, though he dislikes Dr Panna Lal attending on the Professor. It is a homogeneous Muslim group that has gathered at Aziz's; it recites Ghalib and has visions of unity which are shattered by divisions. Aziz takes no interest in politics; though Hamidullah had to attend a meeting of several religious leaders which has been convened to maintain peace and good-neighbourliness. Dr Panna Lal arrives at Major Callendar's request, driven by Ram Chand, to enquire about Dr Aziz. But Dr Panna Lal is irked by the lies spread about Godbole which suggest that the Professor is suffering from cholera. A silly quarrel arises between Ram Chand and Syed Mohammed. Then Cyril Fielding arrives unannounced and the Indians are touched by his kindness. Hamidullah and Fielding get on very well and the Muslim barrister speaks about the existence of a 'beneficent Providence'. The Indians are surprised to know that Fielding does not believe in Providence nor in God and that the West does not bother about belief or disbelief. Is this an index of moral decline? If so, how does England justify her hold on India? Again politics and complexities intrude. Fielding prefers not to answer such questions and seeks refuge in personal relations which matter most to him. The Indian guests slowly file out of Aziz's room.

NOTES AND GLOSSARY

Primus:	a kerosene or paraffin stove. Primus is a trade-name for these stoves
Ghalib:	well-known Urdu and Persian poet (1796-1869) of the nineteenth century, a master of Urdu lyrics
Moslems:	Mohammedans, followers of the Islamic faith
Sikhs:	followers of Sikhism, a religious sect founded by Guru Nanak
Jain:	followers of Jainism, a religious creed founded about 500BC.
Native Christian:	an Indian Christian

Chapter 10

With the approach of summer, weather in India becomes oppressive for men, especially the English who are used to cool weather. Many Indians do not seem to mind how India is governed, just as the lower classes in England do not seem to be much concerned about their country. In the hot weather the indifference of men seems quite pervasive. April seems to be a herald of horror. The sun seems powerful but without beauty or glory.

NOTES AND GLOSSARY

Salaaming:	saluting, bowing

Chapter 11

Fielding wishes to leave but is asked to stay. Aziz then shows him his dead wife's photograph, a rare privilege. Fielding is very pleased with this kind gesture. Aziz says that what Indians need most is kindness and more kindness: 'I assure you it is the only hope.' Would this kindness be adequate to cement Indo-English relations? Would it not need something more than this abstract feeling? Would it not require passion and a little 'intoxication of the blood?' Fielding begins to wonder and comes to realise his own limitations. He is incapable of feeling any intimacy with anyone. Aziz is shocked to hear that Fielding cares neither for marriage nor for children. Fielding abhors the suggestion that he might 'marry Miss Quested', who is a prig. He is shocked by

Aziz's voluptuousness in talking about Adela's breasts or about 'a lady with breasts like mangoes' (p.118). Fielding does not care about the Anglo-Indian Club and its tribal ethic. Nor does he care for his job because he prefers 'to travel light.' He declares that he is 'a holy man minus the holiness' (p.119). His aim in life is to educate people, to make them aware of their individuality, their identity, the sanctity of their personal relations. As Fielding outlines his informal credo, Aziz realises that here is a truly warm-hearted, unconventional and affectionate Englishman who will be friendly with him. Thus the friendship between Aziz and Fielding records its finest moment.

NOTES AND GLOSSARY

saddhus: saintly persons who have renounced material comforts

Part II: CAVES

Chapter 12

The Ganges, which flows from the Himalayas into the plains, is India's greatest and most sacred river. Mythologically it is believed to flow from the hair of Siva (a god of the Hindu triad). However, neither the Himalayas nor the Ganges with its tributaries are as old as the southern part of the Indian peninsula. As Himalayan India emerged out of the sea, the primal India was depressed. This land is so ancient that it represents the earliest geological formation in India. If the flesh of the sun's body is to be found anywhere, it is here—in the antiquity of the Marabar Hills. These hills seem to be outposts of a rising mass of the earth, very abrupt and disproportionate. They are beyond speech and description—they seem 'uncanny'. They are unique and extraordinary. Their uncanny quality smacks of ghosts but they are beyond spirit. Hinduism or Buddhism might have merely scratched their exterior for they are older than spirit and religion.

The Marabar Cave has a five-foot wide tunnel which leads to a chamber of twenty-foot diameter. This pattern is repeated in several formations. These caves are beyond the bounds of sentimental attachment. 'Nothing attaches to them' and they seem to whisper the word 'extraordinary' to mankind.

The caves are dark, and no visitor can see anything unless he strikes a match. The walls of the cave are polished, and the visitor sees another flame rising from the wall; the two flames cannot become one. The flame of the matchstick expires and darkness returns. The chambers are polished, but the tunnels are not. These chambers seem complete cavities; nothing is inside them. They suggest nothing; no morals subsist either. They are absolutely hollow. The *Kawa Dol* cave has a big boulder, and it shakes as a crow perches on it. Hence the name: the *Kawa Dol* (*Kawa* meaning crow, and *dol* meaning swing).

NOTES AND GLOSSARY

Vishnu: the second member of the Hindu Trinity (Brahma, Vishnu and Siva), called the Preserver. His incarnation is Lord Krishna

Siva's: Siva is the third Hindu god, the destroyer

Dravidia: Southern India. The Dravidians were driven to the south by the Aryans in ancient India

Himalayan: of the Himalayas, north India

Bo Tree of Gya: (Bodhi tree) the name given by the Buddhists of India and Ceylon to the pipal (pepul) tree. It was a tree of this species beneath which the Buddha is traditionally supposed to have attained enlightenment at Buddh Gaya, the most important site of Buddhist pilgrimage in India

Kawa Dol: the name of a cave in the Marabar Hills. It has a big boulder which shakes as a crow perches on it

Chapter 13

Aziz is not initially serious about his invitation to the ladies for a visit to the Caves. He has two sorts of memories—one shortlived and the other long lasting—and he has allotted this invitation to his transitory memory. Neither Aziz, nor the two ladies, nor Mr Heaslop is enthusiastic about the picnic, yet it takes place. Aziz makes elaborate preparations for the party. He secures Callendar's permission, Mahmoud Ali's cutlery and other paraphernalia. He is worried over transport arrangements and Godbole's food. He even spends the night on the railway platform supervising the servants and general arrangements. The picnic has cost Aziz a great deal of money. Mrs Moore and Adela arrive punctually and he greets them. The train arrives and the ladies get in. Aziz persuades Adela to send Antony, her servant, back home. They are introduced to Mohammed Latif, a comic, small man. The train starts and Aziz sees Fielding and Godbole held up near a level crossing. They try to get into the train but fail in their efforts. Aziz is upset because Fielding cannot join the party and lend his support. They are on their way to the Marabar and Aziz seems rather worried.

NOTES AND GLOSSARY

a Brahman:	a member of the priestly Hindu caste
guavas:	tropical, edible, pear-shaped fruit mostly used for jellies
Godbole's pujah did it:	the long time taken by Godbole's worship of God resulted in Fielding and Godbole missing the train

Chapter 14

The impact of Godbole's song on the two ladies has been rather peculiar; they live protectively covered 'inside cocoons' (p.133)—and encounter an inner apathy. Adela consciously tries to appear enthusiastic, though the effort does not spring from her heart. She had planned to visit India and observe Ronny under a tropical sky with a view to matrimony. Now that she is in India and also engaged to be married, this prospect should please her, but it doesn't. India on that picnic day seems dim to her, though she is amused by the early experience of the expedition. Mrs Moore and Adela discuss the heat of the Indian weather. Mrs Moore wants to return to England after Ronny's marriage which has been arranged to take place at Simla. Mrs Moore has managed to get Ronny and Adela together but she cannot go further than this and succeed in cementing their bonds.

> She felt increasingly (vision or nightmare?) that, though people are important, the relations between them are not, and that in particular too much fuss has been made over marriage; centuries of carnal embracement, yet man is no nearer to understanding man. (p.135)

The train to the Marabar crosses a nullah and Adela remembers the accident caused by the hyena and the shake up it gave her. The sound of the train—'pomper, pomper, pomper'—reverberates in her ears, but she cannot grasp its message. India, it seems to her, is a vast expanse—villages, farms, hills, streams, large cities. It makes her reflect: 'How can the mind take hold of such a country? Generations of invaders have tried, but they remain in exile' (p.136). India seems incomprehensible to her: 'She (India) is not a promise, only an appeal' (p.37).

The sun rises and Adela is enchanted by the expanding light. However, deep despair ensues from the morning breeze. Is it a false dawn? The Marabar, compared to Grasmere (a wild stretch of the Lake District in northern England) is large, untidy and unmanageable—so it seems to her rational mind. The train stops near the hills and Adela and Mrs

Moore are surprised to see an elephant brought to the place for a ride. This elephant is a majestic part of the picnic and Aziz had to use a great deal of influence before he could obtain the use of it. The guests climb on to the elephant and the ride towards the cave begins. However, the scene is peculiarly ominous:

> As the elephant moved towards the hills (the pale sun had by this time saluted them to the base, and pencilled shadows down their creases) a new quality occurred, a spiritual silence which invaded more senses than the ear. Life went on as usual, but had no consequences, that is to say, sounds did not echo or thoughts develop. Everything seemed cut off at its root, and therefore infected with illusion. (p.140)

Aziz is too preoccupied with his own hospitable sentiments to notice that the atmosphere is infected by subtle despair and danger. He is ignorant of this baffling aspect of primeval India, and cannot really comprehend it or encounter it without the help of Professor Godbole. Professor Godbole, unfortunately, has been left behind: Fielding and he had missed the train because he had miscalculated the length of a prayer!

Mrs Moore and Adela are treated to a sumptuous breakfast, as Aziz tends to overestimate hospitality, mistaking it for intimacy. He recalls his meeting with Mrs Moore in the mosque and the old lady reciprocates his sentiments with a reference to 'Aurangzebe, the Mogul Emperor'. Adela has learnt about the Mogul emperors, particularly Akbar and his new religion (*Din-e-Ilahi*). Aziz does not appreciate Akbar very much ('Akbar is very wonderful, but half a Hindu' (p.145)), but Adela advocates universal brotherhood and a liberal approach to religion:

> 'But wasn't Akbar's new religion very fine? It was to embrace the whole of India.'
> 'Miss Quested, fine but foolish. You keep your religion, I mine. That is the best. Nothing embraces the whole of India, nothing, nothing, and that was Akbar's mistake.' (p.145)

She tells Aziz that she will marry Mr Heaslop and underscores her difficulty in getting adjusted to the Anglo-Indian ethos primarily because she is so different from the general type of Anglo-Indian woman.

Mrs Moore and Adela, along with others, enter the first cave and see a small black hole. The cave seems primeval, and the precipices bland and bald. Did the planet look thus before man's coming? It gives a horrid feeling to Mrs Moore. She nearly faints in it partly because it is overcrowded by visitors. Mrs Moore loses sight of Aziz and Adela in the dark and 'some vile, naked thing' strikes her face. She hits her head in a fit of madness and hears a fearful echo. Godbole has not talked of any echo at all. The Marabar echo is without distinction, monotonous, dull:' "Boum", "bou-oum," or "ou-boum,"—everything, every sound creates the same response, reduced to "boum"! ' There is no evil in the cave, but Mrs Moore feels deeply exhausted. She asks Aziz and Adela to go ahead without her. They go ahead to Kawa Dol and Mrs Moore sinks into a chair. She starts writing a letter to her children 'Dear Stella, dear Ralph,' but communication seems to fail. To her everything seems reduced to nullity. Even the elephant is reduced to nothingness. The echo works on her mind adversely and she loses her will to live:

> Coming at a moment when she chanced to be fatigued, it had managed to murmur, 'Pathos, piety, courage—they exist, but are identical, and so is filth. Everything exists, nothing has value.' (p.150)

The Marabar echo robs infinity of its vastness. Mrs Moore is overtaken with despair. Religion—Christianity—suddenly appears at the edge of her mind and its message 'Let there be light' is drowned in the 'boum'. She is vexed over a large area in the universe which is not comprehensible to her intellect. She is almost dazed with horror. She loses interest in Aziz, in men and the world and surrenders herself to the vision.

NOTES AND GLOSSARY

Aurangzebe: He lived from 1618 to 1707 and was the last of the great Moguls, the Emperors of Hindustan. He was a son of Shah Jehan, who extended the domain of his empire especially in the Deccan, Southern India. Very narrow and fanatical in his attitudes, he alienated the Hindus. The Mogul Empire began to disintegrate rapidly after his death

Akbar: Jalal-ud-din Mohomad (1542–1605), son of Humayun, and grandson of Babur, the founder of the Mogul Empire in India. Akbar laid the foundation of a large and stable empire. Very tolerant in his attitudes, he contracted marital alliances with royal Rajput families. He founded a new religion called *Din-e-Ilahi*, aimed at bringing the Hindus and Muslims together in religious and social harmony

nullah: Hindi word for a stream in a gully

some of the Mogul stuff: various buildings and monuments of Mogul architecture

Taj:	Taj Mahal, built by Shah Jehan, in memory of his consort, Mumtaz Mahal, at Agra in the seventeenth century. A monument in marble, it has great beauty. This mausoleum (built in 1630–48) is the finest example of Indo-Persian art
Grasmere:	part of the Lake District in England

Chapter 15

Aziz and Adela continue their expedition, which becomes tedious and tiring. While Aziz worries over his picnic arrangements, Adela thinks over her impending marriage. She surveys her immediate future life in the context of her and Ronny's limitations. She suddenly asks Aziz whether he has one wife or more. The question shocks Aziz and he enters a small cave to recover.

Chapter 16

Aziz loses contact with Adela and the guide shouts loudly for her. There is no response. Aziz picks up her broken field-glasses. He slaps the guide in anger. However, Miss Quested is not lost. Aziz catches a glimpse of her joining people in a car on the road. Afterwards Aziz returns to the camp and is pleased with Fielding's arrival. Mrs Moore and Fielding are both puzzled by Adela's unexpected departure in Miss Derek's car.

The train arrives and the party, along with the host of servants, returns to Chandrapore. On arrival at the station, Aziz is arrested by Mr Haq, the Inspector of Police. Aziz is deeply shocked, and even tries to run away; but he is taken to prison.

NOTES AND GLOSSARY

Chin-chin:	An Anglo-Chinese phrase of salutation
M.L.'s:	these are the initials of Mohammed Latif, Aziz's relative

Chapter 17

The Collector, Mr Turton, has watched Aziz's arrest from the waiting room. Fielding is prevented from accompanying Aziz by the authoritarian voice of Mr Turton, who laments that the worst thing in his career has happened, that Adela has been assaulted by Aziz in the cave. Fielding says that this is most improbable and that Miss Quested must be mad to level such a preposterous charge. Aziz surely could not be guilty. Turton, surprised by Fielding's defence of Aziz, asks him to withdraw his remark against Adela. Turton, who claims twenty-five years of administrative experience in the district, spurns the idea of the English and the Indians coming together socially. He approves of 'courtesy', but disapproves of 'intimacy' in such relations. Turton has been dominated by the herd instinct of Anglo-India and yet he cares for facts. His meeting with Fielding terminates on a tense note.

NOTES AND GLOSSARY
punkah: fan
chuprassi: official peon or office attendant

Chapter 18

Fielding meets Mr McBryde, the District Police Officer, who is civilised and reflective. He tells Fielding that Aziz made advances to Adela in the cave and then she hit back at him with her field-glasses. These field-glasses with broken straps have later been found in Aziz's possession. Adela, according to McBryde, suffers from an echo, and has made these statements. She had rushed down through cactuses and Miss Derek had saved her life. She is still suffering from fever and heat. Fielding is told that Aziz will get a fair trial.

NOTES AND GLOSSARY
South of latitude 30: angular distance, measured in degrees
Karachi: industrial city and harbour in Sind, in Pakistan
Mutiny: the widespread revolt of Indian troops against the
                        British power and the East India Company in 1857.
Bhagavad Gita: the most sacred book of Hinduism, part of the
                        Mahabharata, a dialogue between Shri Krishna
                        and Arjuna
Why mix yourself up with pitch?: McBryde advises Fielding not to join
                        the Indian supporters of Aziz. Why should Fielding
                        get involved?

Chapter 19

Fielding meets Mr Hamidullah, the local barrister, who has come to call on Mr McBryde. Fielding is on Aziz's side and is therefore against his own people in the Club. He is told that Amritrao, a Calcutta barrister, will be engaged for Aziz's defence. The situation in Chandrapore is tense.

Fielding has a curious conversation with Professor Godbole, which began as a continuation of the interminable conversation about the Russell's Viper which had been found in a classroom some weeks before. Then Godbole refers to the Marabar expedition and Fielding is eager to know the mystic's reaction to the event. Godbole seems keen on discussing a proper title for a new high school, whereas Fielding is completely preoccupied with Aziz's arrest. He asks Godbole, 'Is Aziz innocent or guilty?' Godbole's answer to this question is couched in philosophical and metaphysical terms. Who had performed this 'act' in the cave? If it was an evil action, it expressed the whole of the universe. Good and evil, he says, are different, but both are aspects of the divine. He asks Fielding whether they have visited the Tank of the Dagger near the caves. Fielding visits Aziz in prison, but the doctor is almost incoherent because of the shock he has experienced. Fielding then writes a letter to Miss Quested, but this is of no avail.

NOTES AND GLOSSARY

Russell's Viper: a poisonous snake, horned and long-nosed

pargana: district or county

Chapter 20

The alleged assault on Adela Quested arouses the group instinct of Anglo-India and brings to the fore the patriotic qualities of the English. The Collector, who has kept his peace, is not unduly worried over this affair or the Mohurram. Fielding and Anglo-India register the parting of their ways, an inevitable consequence of the indictment of Aziz. To Anglo-India, Adela is a victim, Ronny a martyr. The Major makes serious allegations against Aziz at the Club, but these receive no support from Mr Turton. Fielding does not stand as a mark of respect when Heaslop arrives at the Club and also declares unambiguously that Aziz is innocent. He resigns from the Club in a tense situation and this dramatic event is symptomatic of the great gulf between Imperial Anglo-India and Fielding, the liberal individual.

NOTES AND GLOSSARY

Mohurram: A religious ritual of the Shiah sect among Muslims. Shiahs mourn the death of Hasan and Husain, which took place on Kerbela battleground.

tête-à-tête: (*French*) a private, confidential interview or conversation

Gurkha: person of the fighting race of Nepal claiming Hindu origin

Tommies: a generic name for privates in the British Army

Rajputs:	people of Rajasthan known for their valour
Jats:	a caste among the Hindus known for its fighting qualities
Panjabi:	people of the Punjab, the land of the five rivers; they have the reputation of being great fighters
Sikhs:	followers of Sikhism, a religion founded by Guru Nanak
Marathas:	the inhabitants of Maharashtra known for their courage in warfare
Bhils:	strong, sturdy tribal people of Central India
Afridis:	members of the Afridi tribe known for their valour
Pathans:	inhabitants of North-West Frontier Province, now in Pakistan
ottoman:	a kind of divan or couch
quod:	(*British slang*) prison
Monsalvat (Man-o-Salva):	according to the *Quran*, the Holy Book of Islam, the food that fell from Heaven for the Israelites in exile; the same as Manna, mentioned in the Bible (*Exodus*, 16: 15), the food of the Israelites in the wilderness
Walhalla:	Valhalla: In Scandinavian mythology, the hall assigned to those who have died in battle, in which they feast with Odin. A place or sphere assigned to persons, etc. worthy of special honour

---

Chapter 21

After the break with Anglo-India, Fielding explores ways of getting closer to Indians; he sees some Mohurram tigers and tazias. He meets Aziz's friends and discusses with them the issue of the grant of bail for Aziz. He is told that a telegram has been sent to Amritrao, a well-known barrister from Calcutta and that he has agreed to work as a defence lawyer for Aziz. Fielding is inclined to tell Professor Godbole that he has committed a mistake in being rude to Ronny but before he can do so the professor has slipped off to a new job in Mau.

NOTES AND GLOSSARY

Mohurram:	a religious ritual of Shiah Muslims mourning the death of Hasan and Husain, descendants of the Prophet Mohammed
tazia:	structures or floats made of bamboo and paper taken in a procession at Mohurram

Chapter 22

Adela remains in McBryde's bungalow, overtaken by her psychic problem, her peculiar dilemma. For a while she believes that Aziz did not even touch her and then the charge seemed all nonsense. At a later stage she sheds tears and her attempt to 'think the incident out' fails. She suffers from an echo. She thinks of Mrs Moore and worries over the ordeal of the trial.

Adela arrives at Ronny's house, but Mrs Moore is not very helpful, nor is she much involved in the situation. She says she will not take part in any trial, nor will she give evidence. In a tense state, Adela believes that Aziz is innocent and that she has made a ghastly mistake. Later Mrs Moore casually confirms this. However, Adela has started the legal machinery and it must complete its course. Ronny looks into the list of steamer sailings to England. He thinks his mother should leave India and go back home; he feels that she is doing no good to herself or anyone else.

Chapter 23

Lady Mellanby offers a place to Mrs Moore in her own reserved cabin on a P. & O. liner leaving for England. Mrs Moore thus escapes the trial of Aziz, the wedding of Ronny and Adela, and also the hot summer. She had experienced the vision (or anti-vision?) when both the horror and the smallness of the universe came into her ken and she had been involved in a twilight world of double vision. Who exactly spoke to her through the cavity or cave remains unanswerable. Was it the 'undying worm' which dwelt in the cave?

Ronny cannot escort Mrs Moore to Bombay and she travels alone by train, seeing Asigarh from her compartment. What do the caves and Asigarh have in common? She sees a hundred Indians pass before her and the nagging question remains: 'What is India? Is it an echo of the Marabar? Is that the final picture or message of India?' Mrs Moore is faced with the problem of disentangling the hundred Indias that come within her sight. Can the caves be considered representative of India and her civilisation? The answer is that the caves represent only a part of India, and not the whole of that country. This is obvious in the division of the novel itself. 'Temple' is surely another aspect of India.

NOTES AND GLOSSARY

Vindyas: a range of mountains in central India north of Narmada river

Shri Belgola:	name misspelt. This is Shravanbelagola, a very ancient statue of Gommateshwara, a Jain deity of Karnataka
Mandu and Hampi:	Mandu is a town in Madhya Pradesh; once the 'city of Joy', it still breathes an atmosphere of romance. Jal Mahal Palace is located in the fort.
	Hampi was the glorious capital of the Vijayanagar Empire, now in ruins. It is in Karnataka, thirteen miles from Hospet
Khajraha:	spelt as Khajuraho, world-famous erotic carvings of the principal Hindu gods
gardens of Shalimar:	Mogul gardens in Srinagar in Kashmir, known as the 'abode of love'

Chapter 24

The summer heat grows atrocious and men become irritable. Adela, the adherent of intellectualism, seems to return to Christianity. Her mind is foggy and confused and nobody really understands her malady. She asks herself: 'Do I love Ronny? Am I capable of loving anyone?' The echo gets hold of her again.

The trial marks the climax of the crisis between Indian and English people. Mr Das takes Ronny's place as the magistrate. The Turtons, Derek, Lesley and the Major have called on Adela to offer their good wishes and support. The case is announced; the court-room is crowded and very hot. The *punkahwallah*, a small, almost naked man, works the fan; he seems to control the proceedings. Mr M°cBryde laboriously narrates the details of the picnic and how it all began with Fielding's tea. He focuses attention on Aziz's moral lapses. As Adela seems to be about to faint, Mr Das allows her to be seated on the platform. The other Anglo-Indians also take their seats on it, but this is severely objected to by Mr Mahmoud Ali and Mr Amritrao, and Mr Das rules that they must go back to their seats. Thereafter, Adela Quested, too, begins to feel at ease. McBryde continues to present details of the Marabar visit. He draws attention to the broken straps of the field-glasses and connects them to Aziz's alleged assault on Adela. His presentation of the case is interrupted by the mention of Mrs Moore's name and Mahmoud Ali's demand that she be summoned as a witness. He says, 'Give us back Mrs Moore and she will save my friend' (p.225). Then he suddenly leaves the courtroom in a state of agitation, saying that the trial is a farce.

The Indians outside begin to chant 'Esmiss Esmoor!' 'Esmiss Esmoor!'

The real crisis has still to develop. Adela sincerely wishes to explore and tell the truth, and nothing but the truth. Mr McBryde asks her about the situation in the cave where the assault was alleged to have taken place. Did she go alone into the cave? 'Yes,' she replies. 'And the prisoner followed you?' McBryde comes to the crucial point. Adela waits for a while and says:

'I am not—' Speech was more difficult than vision. 'I am not quite sure.' (p.229)

McBryde is taken aback by Adela's answer and tries to reconstruct the scene to elicit a positive answer. Adela then declares that Aziz has never followed her into the cave and that she has made a mistake. The entire superstructure of the prosecution falls in like a pack of cards and McBryde is compelled to withdraw the case.

NOTES AND GLOSSARY

Balder: the god of light and virtue, son of Odin and Frigga in Norse mythology

Persephone: in Greek mythology, a beautiful goddess, the daughter of Zeus and Demeter, who, as she was picking flowers, was carried off by Pluto and made his queen in the lower world

Lakshmi: the Hindu goddess of wealth

sweepers: a community of cleaners in India

punkah wallah: *punkah* means a fan, used in tropical countries to circulate and cool the air in rooms. Before electric fans came into use, there were ordinary fans pulled with rope by a servant, called a *punkahwallah*

Raj: sovereignty, rule, kingdom

Chapter 25

Adela has renounced 'Anglo-India', her own people, and paved the way for Aziz's victory. She walks about aimlessly after the recantation and meets Fielding, who escorts her to his place. They are taken in a procession by students, who pull their carriage. Fielding brings Adela to his office and assigns her a couple of rooms. It seems such a queer victory. Aziz joins Fielding, and his Muslim friends wish to celebrate the victory. The crowd, keen on revenge, marches to the hospital to rescue Nureddin. News of his torture has already spread, but this ugly situation is averted by Dr Panna Lal. The Nawab Bahadur (who now wishes to be known as 'plain Mr Zulfiqar') makes a speech about Courage and Prudence, and life seems peaceful again. The crisis is over.

NOTES AND GLOSSARY

sais:	horsekeeper, attendant, groom
victoria:	a low four-wheeled horse-drawn carriage with seats for two persons
splash-board:	board protecting riders on a vehicle from being splashed in wet weather
landau:	a four-wheeled carriage
tatties:	screens made of dried *tad* leaves or khus-khus
hakim:	Hindi word for a physician
Bastille:	the prison fortress built in Paris in the fourteenth and destroyed in the eighteenth century in the French Revolution

Chapter 26

Later Fielding has many talks with Adela because he wants to know the truth of her 'accusation' and 'recantation'. She says she was unwell and that she suffered from an echo. After the recantation, the echo had vanished. Probably she had hallucinations and broke the strap herself. She felt she was sick since the tea party. Adela has been up against something supernatural and doubts the efficacy of rationalism.

Hamidullah arrives and the discussion takes an awkward turn. He is bitter over Aziz's misery and humiliation. Fielding decides that Adela should stay in the college and not go to the Dak Bungalow. Meanwhile Ronny arrives with the sad news that Mrs Moore had died during the voyage near Aden. Adela has a brief talk with Ronny and decides to stay in Fielding's house. The news of Mrs Moore's death silences Hamidullah and he is reconciled to Adela staying in the college. Fielding leaves his house to join Aziz in the victory celebrations.

NOTES AND GLOSSARY
the Dak Bungalow: a guest house for travellers
band-ghari: a closed horse-carriage

Chapter 27

The victory celebrations consist of a banquet at 'plain Mr Zulfiqar's mansion' and a riotous bonhomie. Aziz wants a long holiday to be financed out of the compensation amount he intends to claim from Adela. The idea horrifies Fielding, who tries to persuade him to give up his claim for compensation, if Adela apologises. Aziz says he will consult Mrs Moore and then decide.

the Lion, the disc of Regulus: Regulus, the Roman general who defeated
        the Punic fleet in 256BC. He was later captured and
        tortured to death
Six Mogul Emperors: Babur, Humayun, Akbar, Jehangire, Shah Jehan,
        and Aurangzebe (who were in power during the
        period from 1483 to 1707)

Chapter 28

Mrs Moore dies in the course of her voyage and her body is lowered
into another India—the Indian Ocean. Lady Mellanby sends a cable
conveying this news. A ghost follows the steamer but doesn't go beyond
the Mediterranean. Mrs Moore's death assumes subtler forms in
Chandrapore. People call her 'Esmiss Esmoor' and legends grow around
her remains. She seems to grow into a cult. Ronny feels grieved over
his mother's death and his conscience seems to prick him that he had
not behaved well towards her.

Adela stays in Fielding's college and feels very lonely and desolate.

Northamptonshire: a county in the Midlands in England famous for its
        boot-making industry

Chapter 29

The Lieutenant-Governor's visit to Chandrapore helps to soften the
effect of the Marabar on various characters. Fielding seems more
involved in Adela's problems. She is the picture of sincerity and humility.
Aziz is friendly towards Fielding, but insensitive towards Adela. Mrs
Moore's death shocks him and eventually he gives up his claim for
compensation.

Fielding gently points out her failings to Adela. She wanted to see
India, and not Indians, and she is incapable of affection or warmth. It
has been a failure of personal relationships. Adela admits her spiritual
tether— 'she was up against something', whereas Mrs Moore knew the
truth. Was it telepathy? It might be, but no one could be sure. Adela
leaves for England. After a brief encounter with Antony, her servant,
she boards the steamer at Bombay. Antony tries to blackmail her,
probably to extort a high tip. He says she is called Fielding's mistress.
Adela has him turned out. A missionary on the ship asks her about the
'call of duty,' which prompts her to think about Mrs Moore's other
children—Ralph and Stella, whom she decides to meet in England.

NOTES AND GLOSSARY

Secretariat:	the offices of the secretary of State for India
necromancy:	the art of revealing future events by calling up and questioning the spirits of the dead
Tunbridge Wells:	a small town near London (where Forster lived in 1898)
Cheltenham:	a town in Gloucestershire in England
L.-G.:	abbreviation of Lieutenant-Governor
the monsoons:	the periodical winds of the Indian Ocean which bring rain
Lesseps statue:	the statue of Ferdinand de Lesseps (1805–94) who raised the capital and carried out the project of the Suez Canal between Port Said and Suez

Chapter 30

Aziz becomes a topical—and typical—local hero and even Mr Das calls on him at the hospital, firstly to get medical treatment and secondly to get a poem for a monthly journal. Hindus and Muslims thus have had an odd *entente*. However, as Aziz thinks over his poem, he returns to his old themes: the decay of Islam and the brevity of love. The poem does not get written—but a vague image of the motherland seems to take shape. Aziz then decides to quit British India and cast his lot with 'Indian India', the states governed by Hindu maharajahs or Muslim nawabs. He has heard that Professor Godbole has left for Mau. Aziz too wants to have another job as he has become disgusted with British India. He also hears that Fielding and Adela have had many evenings together, and this arouses his suspicions.

NOTES AND GLOSSARY

bulbuls:	Hindi word for nightingales
Cordova:	a picturesque city in Spain famous for its Moorish cathedral
Samarcand:	a city in Uzbekistan (USSR), east of Bukhara, famous for its mosques
holidays in Kashmir:	holidays in the Kashmir Valley known for its beauty and cool weather. Aziz is not able to go there because of lack of money
Elephant's Ear:	Indian sweet made of wheat flour, sugar and coconut

Chapter 31

Aziz believes the scandalous story about Adela and Fielding and this
suddenly cools his relations with Fielding. He thinks it a kind of betrayal
of friendship. He mentions to Fielding two scandals in the
town—McBryde and Miss Derek, Fielding and Adela. Fielding slowly
realizes that Aziz himself harbours these suspicions under a friendly
garb but he tells him how 'impossible' this is. Aziz is full of regrets as
he realises the strength of Fielding's protest. Fielding insists on dining
with Aziz, he intends to clear up this atmosphere of suspicion between
them.

Fielding is officially invited to a reception at the Club by Mr Turton
for the Lieutenant-Governor, where he meets Major Roberts, the new
Civil Surgeon, Mr Milner, the new Magistrate, and Mrs Blakiston.
Fielding realises that the officials have changed, but the Club remains
the same, the stronghold of British India. He reflects on the echo and
its implications but it belongs to a different world, one not comprehensible to his rational mind.

Aziz and Fielding discuss poetry and their friendship. Fielding is due
to go to England and Aziz to Mussoorie. Aziz's suspicions about the
possibility of Fielding's marrying Adela are not removed, though their
talk is apparently friendly.

NOTES AND GLOSSARY
almeira: Hindi word for cupboard or wardrobe
durry: Hindi word for mattress

Chapter 32

Fielding sails for England via the Suez Canal. Egypt seems charming
to him. Crete welcomes him. He writes picture post cards to his friends.
He visits Venice and perceives the significance of the Mediterranean
as an area of change from Asia to Europe, from East to West, as a
human norm. He is delighted to see the daisies of June in England.

This chapter is about harmony and civilisation, beauty and peace.

NOTES AND GLOSSARY
San Giorgio: a church in Venice (Italy)
the Salute: the stream at the entrance of the Grand Canal in
                      Venice
St Mark's: a famous basilica in Venice
Pillars of Hercules: the rocks Calpe (now Gibraltar) and Abyla (Centa),
                      on either side of the Strait of Gibraltar, fabled to
                      have been set up by Hercules

Part III: TEMPLE

Chapter 33

Professor Narayan Godbole is described reciting a devotional song in praise of Tukaram, a saint, in a palace corridor at Mau in central India. He has left Chandrapore and become a Minister of Education in this Indian state. The occasion is the Gokul Ashtami festival, the birth of Lord Krishna. The Lord was born at the stroke of midnight and was taken away to Brindavan for fear of being destroyed by Kansa, the killer of children. He is the Lord of the Universe and transcends human processes. The Hindus celebrate the Lord's birth every year and worship a silver image in a shrine. The birth is celebrated with music, cymbals, dancing and much merriment. Godbole's choir is given priority in the celebrations. He and his six companions sing of Tukaram, and not of God. Their triumph seemed a muddle, 'a frustration of reason and form' (p.287).

The image of God is hidden behind rose leaves and other foliage. The place is illuminated by electric lights. The inscriptions hang around; one of them is in 'English', 'God si love.' Godbole begins to clash cymbals and sing the devotional hymns. Mrs Moore chances to come into his mind when he is in such a heated state. He impels her by his spiritual force 'to the area of completeness, not of reconstruction.' He remembers a wasp on a stone; he tries to guide the wasp too to achieve the place where completeness can be felt, but fails to move the stone to do likewise. This is a kind of spiritual trance connected with Mrs Moore.

The old, infirm Rajah comes to observe the birth ceremony. Shortly before midnight a Brahmin brings out a wooden model of Gokul and places it near the altar. 'Infinite Love' takes the shape of Lord Krishna. The birth is followed by much merriment. Godbole carries a red napkin before the Rajah who names it 'Shri Krishna'. The Rajah is ill and is being treated by Dr Aziz. Tears pour from his eyes as he is deeply touched by the ceremony. In the sacred corridor, merriment becomes part of the rituals. Butter lumps are exchanged in a spirit of frolic. It is all divine humour: 'God si love.' God plays practical jokes on Himself. They fondle the lordly baby. Perhaps birth becomes an allegory!

Godbole sees Mrs Moore in his vision again. She shares his divine love. He is a Brahmin, she a Christian ... but these divisions are obliterated by his sense of divine unity and universal love. Is she a trick of memory or a telepathic plea? His duty and desire lead him to place himself in a divine posture and say to God, 'come, come, come ...'

This may seem imperfect, but he does what he can. He is trying to bring her to an area where 'completeness' can be found.

NOTES AND GLOSSARY

Kansa: Indian king of Mathura. He had killed seven children of Devaki, Krishna's mother. Krishna was the eighth child, who escaped from this disaster. Krishna later killed Kansa

oleographs: prints in oil-colours or imitations of oil paintings

'Nights of Gladness': the words of the song played by the band

Pandava: the sons of Pandu are Pandavas who ruled Delhi (Hastinapur) and were involved in a war with Kauravas. Their war is the theme of the Indian epic, the *Mahabharata*

Chapter 34

Aziz and Godbole meet for a while. The pious Brahmin informs the Muslim doctor that Fielding, accompanied by his wife, has arrived at the Guest House. Even the thought of Fielding disturbs Aziz's mind. Fielding is on an official tour of schools and colleges in that area. Aziz likes Godbole immensely; he owes his new job in Mau to this pious man. Aziz suspects that Fielding has married Adela. He had never opened his letters because his earlier plea for not claiming damages from Adela had made him suspicious. Aziz's movements in Mau are watched by the British Political Agent, Colonel Maggs, but nothing incriminating is found against him. Godbole tells Aziz that he should meet Fielding since he himself is busy with his religious ceremonies. The thought of Adela's treachery makes Aziz furious and raises a barrier between him and Fielding.

Aziz feels he is an Indian at last; he now hated the English, in the form of Anglo-India and Fielding, his old friend, seemed to have deceived him. His new position and new marriage have changed him.

NOTES AND GLOSSARY

Brahman: member of the Hindu priestly caste

Plassey: The Battle of Plassey (1757) where the English under Lord Clive defeated Siraj-ud-Daulah in Bengal

bhakti: one of the principal pathways to God based on love

Hindi: the major language of India, now recognised as an official or link language.

Sanskrit: the classical language of the Aryans.

Political Agent: the Representative of the Viceroy in an Indian state ruled by native rulers

polity: political organisation, administrative machinery

State Guest House: Government resthouse for guests

Chapter 35

Long ago a young Muslim at Mau, obeying his mother's instructions, had gone to the fort and freed prisoners. The police were annoyed and cut off his head. His resting ground—his burial has now become a shrine—is the 'Shrine of the Head' in a garden.

The bees are about in the garden where Aziz and his children have gone for a stroll. It is a lovely rainy season. Ahmed and Karim run over the grounds shouting joyfully. One prisoner is to be released to celebrate the event of the original liberator. Aziz decides to go to the Mau tank and to the other end of the lake where the Guest House is located. People enquire after the Rajah's health. He is dead, but the news has not been revealed, since it might disturb the festivities.

Fielding and his brother-in-law enter the octagon, but are pursued by the bees. They run in utter confusion. In such an odd situation, Fielding meets Aziz, who offers to send an embrocation. 'Why have you not answered my letters?' Fielding asks him. They talk about the Guest House facilities and the procession. Fielding realises that Aziz has misunderstood him, believing that he has married Adela. In fact he has married Stella, Mrs Moore's daughter. Aziz quarrels with Fielding, but he is excited by the very name—Mrs Moore. It pleases him.

NOTES AND GLOSSARY

pujah: Hindi word for worship of God

sari: traditional dress worn by Indian women

Durbar: the court of the Maharajah

Chapter 36

The festival of Krishna's birth is followed by a procession. There is also a dramatic performance followed by the prince's tribute to the actors. Religion, it seems, is a living force which obliterates many divisions. It creates a pure and pious atmosphere, however transitory it may be.

The palanquin procession begins its march. Aziz and Godbole meet again; it seems the mystic had indeed known of Fielding's marriage to Stella. Aziz feels like a baby in Godbole's presence. The Sweepers'

Band gives a signal for the start. The scene is magnificent. The palanquin moves, the elephants move, the crowd surges ahead. Aziz rides on horseback and sees the great Mau tank. He observes the Guest House and also the Englishmen boating in the tank. Aziz enters the Guest House and secretly reads two letters which give him news about Ronny, Ralph and Adela. The Englishmen are obviously trying to get over their differences and difficulties. Ralph arrives and Aziz examines his bee-stings. Ralph tells him that his hands are unkind. He learns that Fielding and Stella have gone boating.

The state guns boom and the prisoner is released. God extends His temple and the message of salvation reaches the Guest House. The processionists are chanting 'Radhakrishna, Radhakrishna'. The choir creates harmony between Aziz and Ralph and he calls the young Englishman 'an Oriental'. They remember Mrs Moore and Aziz is deeply touched. This marks the beginning of another cycle, and Aziz takes Ralph out on the water.

This is an act of homage to Mrs Moore's son. They row on the lake, see the Fieldings and also the procession. The glare of torches blinds Aziz's eyes.It is windy once again and the boats collide. Stella hurtles into her husband's arms and then dashes against Aziz and causes the boat to capsize. They plunge into shallow water and seem united in peace and harmony. This is a crescendo and a climax of noise and confusion. Godbole smears his forehead with mud which had been adhering to the village of Gokul; the procession ends; the crowds return and the hour is immortalised by 'God si love'. However, nobody can comprehend its emotional centre.

NOTES AND GLOSSARY

Indra:	the principal god of the Hindus, the lord of the Heaven
Krishna:	Lord Krishna who was born on Gokul Ashtami day
Sweepers' Band:	This is a band composed of 'untouchables'
palanquin:	covered litter for one person or a box borne on poles on men's shoulders
Emperor Babur:	Babur (1483–1530), the founder of the Mogul Empire in India
chhatri:	a commemorative monument or shrine
Ganpati:	an Indian god, the son of Siva and Parvati. He has an elephant's head

Chapter 37

The clouds of misunderstanding between Aziz and Fielding are cleared by this experience. They become friends again, although they know that they will meet no more. Realising this, they go on their last ride together in the jungle of Mau. Fielding's visit is not successful; he can't meet· Godbole, nor can he visit the George Fifth High School. In fact, the school isn't started at all. The funny shipwreck has transformed Aziz; he even writes a letter to Adela Quested. Fielding talks about Stella and how their uncertain relationship has been settled by the incident in the Mau tank, which cured her strange troubles. Stella and Ralph seem to like Hinduism, says Fielding. Aziz and Fielding, on their last ride, begin to wrangle over Indo-English politics: Fielding is no longer apologetic about the British Empire in India, whereas Aziz declares that the British in India are of no use. Aziz tells Fielding that the British should clear out of India as quickly as possible. Fielding jeeringly asks whether Indians would then welcome the Japanese, and Aziz mockingly answers, 'Afghans'. Later Aziz cries, 'No foreigners of any sort! Hindu and Muslim and Sikh and all shall be one! . . .'

Fielding mocks these nationalist claims but Aziz continues to say 'Down with the English! . . .' He says that at least his sons will drive the British out of India! And once this is accomplished, 'You and I shall be friends.' Fielding, still dominated by the charm of personal relations, wishes their relationship to develop: 'It's what I want. It's what you want' (p.325).

But neither the horses, nor the earth, nor the sprawling countryside of Mau want it. They declare in their manifold voices, 'No, not yet,' and the sky says, 'No, not there' (p.325).

NOTES AND GLOSSARY

Gokul Ashtami:	the birthday of Lord Krishna in Gokul (8th day of Shravan in Hindu calendar)
Caaba of Union:	Caaba is the Mohammedan sanctuary in the holy city, Mecca, in Saudi Arabia
Hanuman:	the Hindu god, the worshipper of Shree Rama
Saivite temple:	the temple of Siva, of the Saivite sect of the Hindus
peer:	equal in rank
the Holy Roman Empire:	The later Roman Empire with the ideal of the Emperor as defender of the Christian faith. However, some feel it to be an empty title. From the seventeenth century to the extinction of the title in 1806, the Holy Roman Empire was, as Voltaire remarked, neither holy nor Roman

Part 3

Commentary

The title

Forster has stated that he took his title *A Passage to India* from Walt Whitman's well-known poem 'Passage to India' (1871). The great American poet was seeking a passage to more than India, a passage of soul to primal thought, of man to the seas of god. He was proclaiming that:

Nature and Man shall be disjoin'd and diffused no more,
The true son of God shall absolutely fuse them.   (lines 114–15)

Mrs Moore, while observing the Ganges in the moonlight, has a vision of becoming one with the universe. Forster adds the indefinite article 'A' thereby stressing the individuality, the distinctive identity of his quest for the reality of India. Both Whitman and Forster seek the spiritual essence of their experience, though the mode of their quest is clearly governed by the different art-forms they use. While Forster wants to express his search by exploring and extending the form of fiction, Whitman used poetry for expressing it which was philosophical, panoramic, moral, romantic, and highly symbolic. Although the objectives of their quests appear similar, it is clear that their subject-matter and substance, modes and methods are widely divergent. Forster's 'passage' to India is primarily a personal, political, liberal, religious, and spiritual mode which reflects his own quest for vision and form.

The structure

The structure of *A Passage to India* is three-fold; it is composed of three dominant metaphors: 'Mosque', 'Caves' and 'Temple'. These three sections of the novel have their narrative as well as symbolic substances and meanings. Forster's imagination has quite often been kindled by the concept of three-fold structural patterns. The artistic-spiritual journey toward India takes place through Mosque, Caves and Temple, which are places of worship or primal abodes. Caves are primal abodes because man in his primitive state lived in them. They are metaphors projecting religious and spiritual meanings. For instance, 'Mosque' is associated with arch (the three arcades of the mosque where Aziz sat),

'Caves' with echo, and 'Temple' with sky. These symbols have positive as well as negative connotations and contexts. The positive meaning of the Mosque symbol consists of the possibilities of friendship between Aziz and Fielding, and Aziz and Mrs Moore, whereas the note of negation of these possibilities is struck by the Bridge Party. The episodes in 'Mosque', then, bring peoples of different cultures and religions together, and they also alienate them from each other. The failure of the Bridge Party is an ironic commentary on the attempt to forge a link of friendship between east and west, India and Anglo-India, the ruler and the ruled. Although the symbolic implications of the Marabar Caves are shrouded in mystery or muddle, their interpretations have both positive and negative aspects. This crucial problem is discussed at length in the interpretations of Mrs Moore's and Adela's experiences in the Caves (see pp.60–2 of these notes). The symbol of 'Temple' and 'sky' signifies reconciliation and harmony, although its effect is not enduring. The divisions of daily life seem to reassert themselves. Thus, the dualisms of Forster's values, of earth and sky, heaven and hell, this world and the other, invest the three metaphors with positive as well as negative meanings and an air of uncertainty, of ambivalence ('Outside the arch there seemed always an arch, beyond the remotest echo a silence') seems to prevail.

Another interpretation of the structure of *A Passage to India*, offered by George H. Thomson,* shows 'Mosque' as a prelude to the principal issues, 'Caves' as a physical and spiritual waste-land and 'Temple' as an escape from it, supported by a promise of spiritual fulfilment. Again these three sections of *A Passage to India* are believed concurrently to symbolise the three stages of mankind's spiritual history and development. The first stage is represented by a superficial optimism, the second by disillusionment and despair, and the third by a qualified spiritual achievement. These three stages in *A Passage to India* are represented by, and embodied in Aziz, Mrs Moore and Godbole.

The image of India, a land of immense geographical, religious, racial, linguistic and cultural diversities is central to the structure of *A Passage to India*. Forster projects the various degrees of comprehension of this image by the principal characters, Aziz, Fielding, Adela, Mrs Moore and Godbole. India in Forster's *A Passage to India* is thus a microcosm of the universe itself. Mrs Moore on her return journey looks at Asirgarh and the palm trees near Bombay: 'Perhaps the hundred Indias which fuss and squabble so tiresomely are one, and the universe they mirror

*George H Thomson, *The Fiction of E.M. Forster*, Wayne State University Press, Detroit, 1967, pp.201–2.

is one.' The threefold structure, of 'Mosque', 'Caves' and 'Temple' encompasses the varied symbolic and religious layers of the universe which Forster creates in his novel.

The structure of *A Passage to India* has another level of significance which is climatic, seasonal, of nature. Forster in the 'Author's Notes' refers to the 'three seasons of the Indian year—winter, summer, and the rains' which are coextensive with the three sections and provide a significant setting which suits the narrative, dramatic and symbolic patterns of *A Passage to India*. It is this association of the Indian seasons and nature with the three sections that strengthens the concepts of the wasteland and fertility in understanding the final meaning of *A Passage to India*.

Elements of vision

The question of the form or structure of *A Passage to India* must not be isolated from its vision, the imaginative quality implicit in it. Forster's imagination is evoked by a strange country in the east with its own traditions of religion and culture. For instance, Godbole's conversation with Fielding about the Hindu view of God sounds strange to him. Godbole's God encompasses good and evil and He is thus all-inclusive. The moral differences between good and evil, so significant to Christianity, are thus transcended by Godbole's utterances. Forster's own statement shows that the Marabar Caves suggest a world robbed of its spirit. It is a godless universe. However, Godbole's views, as shown by Forster, indicate the complexity of this problem: God's absence need not imply His non-existence. Therefore, Godbole is entitled to ask for divine blessings, 'Come, come, come, come.'

Godbole's ideas, attitudes and behaviour are also connected with what he thinks of Mrs Moore and her experiences. Did Mrs Moore see desolation, death and decay? Or did she visualise a better universe? Was her vision of life and the world positive or negative? These are obviously difficult questions. Mrs Moore is important in herself. However, Forster presents her not merely as she is, but as she appears in Godbole's imagination. It is through his eyes that we are made aware of her dispositions, desires and dilemmas.

In the third section, while dancing before God, Godbole observes Mrs Moore, and directs her to the position where completeness can be found. The places and persons in *A Passage to India* are thus deeply involved in the quest for unity, of man and nature, man and universe, man and god. Mosque, Caves and Temple are thus not merely parts of a threefold structure, they also convey Forster's all-comprehensive vision. *A Passage to India* thus presents a complete microcosm of Forster's moral, religious and aesthetic design in which the form and structure, vision and design play their part in accentuating man's basic quest for unity, his voyaging toward the sea of God, and his advance toward spiritual fulfilment and fruition.

Mosque, the prelude to *A Passage to India*

The 'Mosque' section opens out the possibilities of friendship and affection between the Indians and the English, which is one of the principal themes of *A Passage to India*. It symbolises the values of Islam, such as the equality of all men and universal brotherhood. Its principal representative is Aziz, a highly emotional person, who believes in the unwritten laws of love. His arrival at and departure from Hamidullah's house are marked by very impulsive responses. His first words spoken to Mrs Moore in the mosque are almost censorious, whereas his later words reflect his genuine affection. He recalls the phrase 'the secret understanding of the heart' with tears in his eyes. His later utterances to Mrs Moore in the mosque ('Then you are an Oriental') are an index of his deep affection and admiration for her and a total reversal of his earlier snarl.

Aziz is primarily an emotional being whose responses to persons and events are quick, unpremeditated, genuinely affectionate or hostile; they emanate from his senses and double memory. He appears to absorb the black and white dualism of the mosque in his consciousness and it affects his mind. In his meeting with Mrs Moore, Aziz freely ventilates his grievances against Major Callendar. Their talk is personal, familiar, intimate, and he is deeply drawn towards her in the quiet atmosphere of the mosque. Forster portrays their meeting with rare delicacy; they appear like two children of God seeking a spiritual communion.

The bonds of kindred spirits are forged in a religious place in familiar atmosphere. The ninety-nine names of God on the frieze and the black and white dualism make a sensitive impression on Aziz's imagination and awaken his sense of beauty. He felt immensely happy in the mosque and so totally absorbed in an intuitive adherence to the Islamic faith—'an attitude towards life both exquisite and durable'—that he seemed to have found and experienced a 'secret understanding of the heart.' The 'heart' is continually emphasised in respect of Aziz because it is the principal guide to his conduct and attitudes. It is the heart and not the brain which seems the main driving force in his personality. Yet he is often confused and up against difficulties with the world. This ambivalent nature of Aziz sets the tone of the uncertain quality of the 'Mosque' section as a whole.

Irony of the 'bridge' between East and West

The Bridge Party, organised by Mr Turton, is an ironic comment on the attempt to make East meet West and explore the areas of friendship. It is a comic reversal of the spirit of the meeting of Aziz and Mrs Moore in the mosque. Forster trenchantly exposes the haughtiness and arrogance of the English ladies, especially Mrs Turton. The Bridge Party does not go beyond formal civilities and surface graces in spite of sincere efforts made by Mr Turton, Mrs Moore, Adela Quested and Cyril Fielding. The Indians are no less responsible than the Anglo-Indians for this dismal failure because they are too self-conscious to share freely in the pleasure of the conversation. Forster's irony is directed as much against the Turtons as against the Bhattacharyas. While Mrs Turton, on being told that the Indian ladies had visited Paris, thought of their movements as if they were migratory birds, the semi-westernised Indian ladies in their anxiety to parade their knowledge of London speak of 'High Park Corner' [Hyde Park Corner]. The Bhattacharyas arrange that Mrs Moore and Adela should visit their home on Thursday and promise to send a carriage. The carriage, of course, never turns up. Englishmen are prevented by their womenfolk from being cordial to the Indians at the Bridge Party, and this partly explains its failure. All invitations to such attempts at union 'must proceed from heaven perhaps' (p.35), but they do not. It is futile for Turtons and Burtons, Adelas and Fieldings, Azizes and Godboles to initiate their own attempts at unity. The Club itself seems a kind of a heaven where, in the words of Mrs Moore, 'Englishmen like posing as gods' (p.48). The Bridge Party indeed seems one of Turton's 'tiresome' jokes—superficial in substance and futile in effect. It is only a social and racial correlative of the effort toward spiritual unity, a kind of parallel to the main theme of unity of the novel.

The Bridge Party becomes an ironic symbol of man's indifference to man, set against the wider horizon of a universe which is open to some and closed to others at the same time. The cosmos is described as a system of orbs or heavenly bodies which is either closed or open. The universe becomes small the moment it is turned into a closed system. It is this smallness of the universe that later becomes part of Mrs Moore's 'Double Vision'.

Fielding's tea party and Godbole's song

Whereas the Bridge Party was a failure of Anglo-Indian bureaucracy, Fielding's tea party, which proceeded from it, is a subtler kind of failure.

It is a small and civilised group bound by mutual respect and similar cultural values. Aziz is at his best and his imagination soars on great wings while talking about the Moguls and their times. He has already established a quick, easy, genuine rapport with Fielding, while Mrs Moore and Adela both find him charming. He speaks about the Mogul skills of water supply and his statement is unscientific, but he does not care for verbal truth at all. He is merely concerned with the truth of a particular mood.

The conversation of Mrs Moore, Adela, Aziz and Godbole seems light and friendly, but it has a strange undercurrent caused by the reference to the Marabar Caves. Aziz has casually invited the ladies to his home, but soon realizes that his invitation has been taken seriously. Realising that his bungalow is a horror, he therefore cries, 'I invite you all to see me in the Marabar Caves' (p.72). Aziz, then, attempts to explain what the Caves were, but he cannot. The 'comparatively simple mind of the Mohammedan is [was] encountering Ancient Night' (p.74) or primeval darkness. Even Professor Godbole cannot succeed in explaining what the Caves were about and his answers seem negative—or perhaps he is concealing something. The mere reference to the Marabar opens the doors of disaster. Ronny arrives and his unintended rudeness wrecks the entire evening. He ignores Aziz who provokes him, and the odd, almost melodramatic, scene of leave-taking begins. Everyone says 'Good-bye' in a moment of irritation and frustration. In a situation when everyone is cross and wretched, Professor Narayan Godbole sings a song about Lord Krishna and his *gopis*.

The subject-matter of the song is fairly clear, but its interpretation, and particularly its functioning, are shrouded in mystery. The theme of the song is the desire of the milkmaiden—the *gopi*—to attain communion with her Lord, Krishna. It dramatises the woman's self-surrender to her Lord in love, which is analogous to the devotee's total self-surrender to God. Thus, the erotic motif is combined with the divine desire. The milkmaiden worships Lord Krishna and prays, 'Come to me only', but he refuses to come. Mrs Moore queries whether 'He comes in some other song', and Godbole replies, 'Oh, no, he refuses to come.' God's refusal to respond to the call of love sets the tone of the Marabar disaster.

The theme of the song is love and self-surrender, a universal passion of Indian devotional poetry. Its genesis may be traced to the *bhakti* cult which has dominated poetry in Indian languages for a long time. The *bhakti* cult is a pathway to God based on love and passion. There are three specific and well-ordered pathways to God in Hinduism: the path of Knowledge, the path of Work and the path of Love. Godbole's song comes into the third category which also highlights the combination of the erotic with the divine in a mystical sense. The *gopis* pray their lord to come to them without realising the divine truth that God is within them, within their divine soul. They feel, however, that he refuses to come and this realisation leads to the concept of the Godless universe of Marabar Caves.

Godbole's song is neither a mere comic episode nor a digression. It is not functionless. It is a part of a stream of events, the subtle pattern of voices which seems to affect the minds of the principal characters in the book. Forster unfolds this effect in a significant comment:

> Ever since Professor Godbole had sung his queer little song, they had lived more or less inside cocoons, and the difference between them was that the elder lady accepted her own apathy, while the younger resented hers.(p.133)

This queer song exercises a subtle influence on the consciousness of both Mrs Moore and Adela Quested. Obviously, the meaning of the song is related to their personal predicaments in a universe which is beyond the boundaries of rational comprehension. Godbole's silence on the implications of the Caves, culminating in the subtle undercurrent of the song is a masterstroke of Forster's understatement. One of the many facets of the complexity of Mrs Moore's experience is revealed in the small accident to the Nawab Bahadur's car on the Marabar Road. It was probably a hyena that had dashed against the car. But, Mrs Moore, on being told of it, exclaims that it was a ghost. Strangely enough, the Nawab Bahadur too imagines that it was a ghost of a man whom he had run over years ago. The man, it seemed, had been waiting at that spot to kill the Nawab Bahadur. This stream of events only adds to the subtleties of the narrative structure of the novel and its deeper, psychic implications.

The Marabar Caves

Although many critics agree that the Marabar Caves are the main symbol in *A Passage to India*, interpretations of their function and meaning are widely diverse. The visit to the Caves is the central episode in *A Passage to India*, but this visit has been subjected to a bewildering variety of interpretations. No literary critic who has tried to enter these Caves in an attempt to trace the footprints of Mrs Moore, Adela and Aziz and explain their significance has escaped unscathed. Whether the Marabar in *A Passage to India* is a mystery or a muddle or a peculiar combination of both will remain a subtle and elusive problem.

What happened in the Caves? Some probable answers

What actually happened in the Marabar Caves and how and why it affected the minds of Mrs Moore and Adela are indeed very complex questions. The experiences of these two Englishwomen and their precise interpretations seem to elude neat analysis. Undoubtedly Mrs Moore suffered a spiritual and also a physical breakdown. She was a religious mystic who aimed at becoming one with the universe. She wished to communicate with God but finally ended up with a total loss of desire; she took a pencil and paper for writing a letter but could not proceed beyond 'Dear Stella ... Dear Ralph ...' She had earlier envisioned a universe bound together by a unity of man and nature. Later the Marabar spoke to her of a universe without value. Even the moral categories, of good and evil, were destroyed and 'Nothingness' prevailed. Mrs Moore was overtaken by a profound despair and lost her will to live. The echo appeared to end everything for her. The mood which had dominated her in the last two months at last took shape, and she was confronted with the universe without value, of utter Nothingness. This is one of the interpretations of Mrs Moore's experience and the happenings in the Caves.

Secondly, the Caves seem to be symbolic of the principal theme of *A Passage to India*, of the barrier between unity and separation, matter and essence, India and Anglo-India. In the primitive state of man caves functioned in a dual way: they were his shelter and also his tomb. Men, after death, were buried in the caves. They also lived in them. This primordial nature of the Caves suggests man's attempt towards unity between the material and the spiritual and is reflected in the significant scene of the two flames. The Caves thus symbolise man's attempt towards universal unity as well as the fact of his mortal being, death as a fact of life. Mrs Moore, who later dies, represents this death-aspect of the primordial caves. The small black hole in the Cave similarly stands for the act of dying, which is further accentuated by the atmosphere of darkness. Thirdly, Mrs Moore underwent a soul-shattering experience in the Marabar Caves. The Caves represent several complex facets of Indian thought, such as the 'impersonal cosmic principle,' the total 'renunciation,' the 'Void' in Buddhism, the dichotomy or division between spirit and matter, the undifferentiated 'Oneness of the Absolute.'

Mrs Moore's experience may be religious as she has a vision of the vast immensity of the Timeless Absolute which the Caves signify. In consequence, the inherited values of her Christian faith are annihilated and she is shown as pondering over 'poor little talkative Christianity' (p.150). Mrs Moore died in the course of her sea voyage; her body was lowered into the sea and a ghost followed the ship up the Red Sea but did not enter the Mediterranean. She underwent a strange transformation in that the Indian people began to chant 'Esmiss Esmoor' outside the courtroom at Aziz's trial. This itself is a peculiar 'echo' emerging from the unconscious stream of events in the book.

Mrs Moore had probably planned a retreat into her own cave-like self, the unconscious, psychic state in which the horror and the smallness of the universe would become simultaneously visible to her. This twilight world is dominated by despair, by the 'Ancient Night' of the Caves. She becomes a legend in India and finally she, or her image, enters the visionary mind of Godbole and is united with him in search of wholeness and unity, the all-inclusive love for all men, for animate and inanimate beings.

Adela Quested's experience in the Caves

The reader may well ask what in fact did happen in the Caves? The answer may be: Nothing—and, perhaps, Everything. From Nothing to Everything includes the vast area—from negation to all inclusive unity.

A subsidiary, yet very significant, question arises about Adela's experience in the Caves. What is most likely to be the nature and quality of her experience? She is, primarily, a product of Christian rationality and Anglo-Saxon common sense. Like Fielding, she seems to lack religious faith, and this makes her unequal to the task of realising the religious predicaments of the Caves. On entering the caves, she begins to consider her personal problems, her marriage to Ronny, a kind of union which seems to her without love or real involvement. She then observes the 'double row of footholds' in the rock which remind her of the danger of marrying without love, of pure animal instincts dominating life's major choices.

She begins reflecting on the marriage and the Marabar strikes its gong, making her aware of the hollowness of that union. Marriage without love is tantamount to rape: this is a feeling in her unconscious mind and it explains why she levels the charge of assault against Aziz. Another interpretation of Adela's experience, and specially of the fantastic charge that she brings against Aziz, is rooted in a psycho-analytical, almost Freudian, interpretation of her state of being. We may repeat the question: What did happen to Adela in the Cave? The answer: Nothing. And, yet, something of a psychic shock did happen. Both these answers are partly true. Because, at the time Adela received the impact of the echo, she was alone in the cave, and surely Aziz was not there at all. He had entered another Cave for a smoke and to recover his balance. And yet Adela, who was quite a sincere girl, levelled the fantastic charge of indecent assault against him. The main question is: Why did she indulge in such a false, unbelievable indictment?

What is it that Adela really encounters in the Cave? Louise Dauner* suggests that what Adela is up against is—in terms of the theories of the 'animus'—the male consciousness that woman embodies within her. Wilfred Stone† thinks that it is the Jungian 'shadow', the dark depth of the unconscious which strikes horror in Adela's being. The process is very similar to that of a human being passing through a narrow passage—in Adela's case, the Cave—where she meets herself as 'something other'—the shadow. The echo, in actuality, is the sound that erupts from this shadow. It is a crisis of identity, the problem of knowing oneself, the reality of one's being—and Adela is deeply shocked to realise the truth that she does not love Ronny at all, and that her marriage would be a superficial and unreal coexistence.

Secondly, Adela's experience may be interpreted as an encounter with the Cave of Illusion, which is similar to the Cave that the Greek philosopher Plato described in the seventh book of *The Republic*. Adela, it appears, realises the illusory nature of her proposed union and her running away from the Cave is analogous to her flight from stark reality.

Thirdly, what Adela experiences in the Caves is the dualism between intellect and intuition. No person can realise the truth if he observes it only through his intellectual eye or only through some mode of sensory perception. Adela does precisely this; her being is dominated by her rationality and her response to life by her senses. Both these modes of perception are false and she suddenly realises this falsity in the Caves. Thereafter she runs away from the Cave which suggests her rejection of these false values.

Fourthly, another strange interpretation of Adela's charge against Aziz has been offered. It appears that Adela, in her subconscious, wishes to be raped by man, and the cactuses pricking her body, while she is careering down the hill, illustrate the partial fulfilment of this desire. This physical pricking is something which she inwardly desires and the moment this happens, through cactuses, she believes she has been raped. Hence the charge of rape. The conclusion is that she speaks

*Louise Dauner, 'What happened in the Cave? Reflections on *A Passage to India*', *Modern Fiction Studies*, VII, 3, p.267.

†Wilfred Stone, *The Cave and the Mountain*, Stanford University Press, Stanford, 1966, p.335.

of an assault which she very much wanted to take place, but which, in reality, did not take place at all.

Another aspect of Adela's experience in the Cave is her psychic state of hallucination which implies that she develops an illusion, a feeling of having seen a man who is not actually there. In any event she seems to have lost her sense of perception, a fact which is demonstrated by the broken strap of the field-glasses she has carried with her into the Cave. These broken straps probably symbolise her broken power to perceive the truth, the reality of the situation. She also began to suffer from a terrible echo which took hold of her mind and resulted in creating hallucinations. The echo continued to harass her mind till the trial in the court where she withdrew the charge against Aziz. Then it was suddenly silenced. Obviously, the echo was concerned with her state of mind which could not perceive the truth earlier but suddenly realised it under the impact of Mrs Moore's image.

Adela seems to be a divided self, torn between the forces of reason and passion; and the feeling of assault might have been an inner conflict within her own being. The Cave made her aware of this division within her, and the animal instincts attacked the rationality in her person. Whatever may be the plausible reasoning behind her hallucination and the consequential echo, it is clear that Adela does not possess adequate self-knowledge. Her entry into the Cave implies her getting into the dark chamber of her subconscious mind and the consequent explosion of her rationality.

The character and personality of Aziz

Aziz plays a very significant role in *A Passage to India*; he is one of the three or four main characters in the novel. If *A Passage to India* is regarded primarily as a story of the friendship of Aziz and Fielding, its ups and downs and its finale, then Aziz's position becomes central. However, his role has raised much critical controversy and opinions about it, are, therefore, widely divergent.

The key to Aziz's character is provided by the phrase 'the secret understanding of the heart'. He is a creation of impulse, emotion and instinct. He is a lover of gardens, champak flowers, scraps of Persian poetry. Initially he is not much interested in politics, and the themes that attract his poetic temper are the decay of Islam and the transitoriness of love. He obviously hates his domineering boss, Major Callendar, who treats him badly and summons him to his house only to rebuff him. Aziz is an obedient, Anglicised young man who desires equality with the British in social relations.

Aziz's relations with Fielding are in marked contrast to those with Major Callendar. He has a row with the Major over his visit to the latter's house, and as usual, the boss misunderstands him. Aziz feels that 'the English are a comic institution' (p.52) and he likes 'being misunderstood by them'. Aziz is a competent surgeon and indispensable to the Major in serious cases. Aziz is conscious of his professional skill. He also greatly loved his wife; he avoids attending the Bridge Party because it was being held on the day of the anniversary of his wife's death. Aziz is very sentimental, and, looking at the picture of his dead wife, exclaims, 'How unhappy I am!' (p.55). He was self-confident; yet British officialdom overwhelms him and he has creeping fears. But Aziz's relations with Fielding, especially in the initial phase, are based on mutual understanding, deep fellow-feeling and affection. He gives his collar stud to Fielding at their very first meeting, which shows his helpful, large-hearted attitude. Aziz also loves Fielding's untidiness, his informality, his instinctive responses. He particularly appreciates Fielding's visit to his house to enquire about his health. He shows Fielding his dead wife's photograph, a deeply appreciated gesture.

The Marabar expedition was on a lavish scale and Aziz spent a huge amount of money on providing an elephant at the site and the sumptuous breakfast. Aziz undoubtedly is a generous, large-hearted person, who tends to overrate hospitality. In the course of the trial, Fielding boldly champions Aziz's cause and even breaks away from the Anglo-Indian community and his own countrymen. He also resigns from the Anglo-Indian Club, a strong gesture of his identification with Aziz. Aziz loves him for this fine expression of friendship and invites him to join the victory celebrations.

Aziz was deeply shocked by Adela's charge of assault against him because it meant the end of his reputation. He had intended to be genuinely hospitable and the outcome of it appalled him. Therefore, Fielding's suggestion that he should give up a claim for damages from Adela irks him. He agrees to do so only when Mrs Moore's name is brought in. Aziz's responses to Mrs Moore are marked by deep affection and admiration. She thought Aziz was her genuine friend and he generously responded to all her acts of kindness. Aziz's relations with Mrs Moore right from their first meeting in the mosque have been characterised by a profound understanding of the heart and an inwardly felt sense of involvement and affection.

Aziz also had a great liking for Professor Godbole as an individual and as a pious man devoted to God. Aziz's reaction against Hindus, their music or their way of life is often adverse. Yet after the trial he takes a job in a Hindu state.

Aziz's responses to Fielding undergo a change. Trust is replaced by suspicion. He suspects that Fielding may marry Adela, and he attributes motives to Fielding's suggestion of dropping the demand for damages. Aziz and Fielding are brought together in the scene of the bees. The boating incident helps to clear the air of misunderstanding between them.

However, the last scene of *A Passage to India* shows Aziz and Fielding at a crossroad, their individual, affectionate relations becoming clouded by external political factors and compelling political situations. The history of Indo-English political relations seems to darken the personal relationship between these two affable and loving individuals. It is on this ambivalent note that the Aziz-Fielding relationship seems to come to a close in *A Passage to India*.

Forster's style in *A Passage to India*

Style is the form in which thought is expressed, the 'manner' distinguished from the matter. However, the thing said is not entirely independent of the manner of saying it. Each writer dresses his thought in his own way, and therefore style bears the stamp of his personality. Forster's style in *A Passage to India* is elegant, urbane, rhythmic and fully attuned to the needs of his story and its subject.

Forster's main objective in *A Passage to India* is obviously the expression of the interaction of two cultures, the Indian and the Anglo-Indian or British in the social and political situation of India dominated by the British power. It is primarily this confrontation or conflict of cultures and attitudes that he aims at projecting in a language appropriate to the occasion. In his earlier novels he had treated the theme of connecting the prose and the passion of life, but here in *A Passage to India* he deals with the difficulty of making the connection. The Indians dislike the English; so, too, do the English dislike the Indians. However, people such as Fielding wish to break this barrier and desire to seek friendship. The primary aim of language is communication, but in *A Passage to India*, strangely, the language is made a means of expressing the lack of communication between individuals or groups of men.

Forster also aims at showing how Indians converse among themselves in English, what kind of idiom they use, and how it departs from the norms of the native speakers of English. Then, again, he has to show indirectly how Indians speak in their own languages, which of course have to be rendered in English. Thirdly, he is intent upon highlighting the Anglo-Indian slang, the kind of language that the British used in India in the twenties:

'Miss Quested, what a name!' remarked Mrs Turton to her husband as they drove away. She had not taken to the new young lady, thinking her ungracious and cranky. She trusted that she hadn't been brought out to marry nice little Heaslop, though it looked like it. Her husband agreed with her in his heart, but he never spoke against an Englishwoman if he could avoid doing so, and he only said that Miss Quested naturally made mistakes. He added: 'India does wonders for the judgement, especially during the hot weather; it has even done wonders for Fielding.' Mrs Turton closed her eyes at this name and remarked that Mr Fielding wasn't pukka, and had better marry Miss Quested, for she wasn't pukka.   (p.26)

The use of the Anglo-Indian slang term, 'pukka' reflects the British imperial attitude to life.

Forster presents Aziz's arrival at Hamidullah's in a style which adequately reflects their human relations:

'Hamidullah, Hamidullah! am I late?' he cried.

'Do not apologise,' said his host. 'You are always late.'

'Kindly answer my question. Am I late? Has Mahmoud Ali eaten all the food? If so I go elsewhere. Mr Mahmoud Ali, how are you?'

'Thank you, Dr Aziz, I am dying.'

'Dying before your dinner? Oh, poor Mahmoud Ali!'

'Hamidullah here is actually dead. He passed away just as you rode up on your bike.'

'Yes, that is so,' said the other. 'Imagine us both as addressing you from another and a happier world.'   (pp.7–8)

In this passage Forster wants to portray the social and cultural contexts of Indians coming together for an evening meal. He catches the tenor of conversation of a friendly Indian group in whom the serious and the comic are peculiarly mixed. The banter may appear un-English, but it is the way that some educated Indians spoke English at the time Forster wrote the novel.

At the Bridge Party Mrs Bhattacharya and Mrs Das are introduced to Adela and Mrs Moore by Mr Bhattacharya in a language which bears the stamp of Indian usage:

'The shorter lady, she is my wife, she is Mrs Bhattacharya,' the onlooker explained. 'The taller lady, she is my sister, she is Mrs Das.' The shorter and the taller ladies both adjusted their saris, and smiled. There was a curious uncertainty about their gestures, as if they sought for a new formula which neither East nor West could provide.   (p.40)

The Indian mode of using an extra pronoun is faithfully incorporated in the speech patterns. Again, the Indians are fond of using double adjectives, 'jolly, jolly good,' 'very, very good' as expressions of intensity of feeling and Forster shows this accurately. 'You'll jolly jolly well not forget those caves, . . .' Dr Panna Lal's use of English is sometimes monosyllabic when he enquires about Aziz's health. 'How is stomach? . . . how head?' This seems to be a literal translation of Hindi or Indian expressions and also shows the Indian lack of the definite and indefinite articles, 'the,' and 'a'. The Muslim police inspector praises Fielding for having come to see Aziz during his illness:

> 'It is good of Mr Fielding to condescend to visit our friend,' said the police inspector. 'We are touched by this great kindness.' (p.108)

These civilities and surface graces of Indian speech patterns which seem effusive to the English are faithfully rendered by Forster.

The style which portrays Forster's English characters is sophisticated, logical, urbane and reflects his liberal imagination. Mrs Moore is very polite to Aziz, but he misconstrues her civilities as expressions of profound intimacy. In fact, he applies his own norms to her, which is shown in sentences such as his 'Then, you are an Oriental.' The dialogue between Adela and her servant Antony at the station portrays a facet of Indo-English relations. Aziz tells Adela:

> 'Send back your servant,' he suggested. 'He is unnecessary. Then we shall all be Moslems together.'
>
> 'And he is such a horrible servant. Antony, you can go; we don't want you,' said the girl impatiently.
>
> 'Master told me to come.'
>
> 'Mistress tells you to go.'
>
> 'Master says, keep near the ladies all the morning.'
>
> 'Well, your ladies won't have you.' She turned to the host. 'Do get rid of him, Dr Aziz!' (p.129)

The scene at the station indicates the 'celebrated Oriental confusion' and the speech-patterns unfold the relations between masters and servants.

Forster's style achieves a little poetical quality in the descriptions of natural landscapes or cities, visions or nightmares. But there is no false poetical element in *A Passage to India* primarily because it is a novel about relationships between two or more cultures. His style is rhythmic and words like 'come, come' are often repeated to show this recurrent strain. The measured tones of Forster's style depict the qualities of rhythm, urbanity, precision and elegance.

The image of India

The social image depicted in *A Passage to India* is basically one of schism and division. The English are little gods; they create their own heaven in the exclusive Anglo-Indian Club. Hindus and Muslims are entangled in various forms of social relationships, and create their own little worlds. Friendships are formed and forged, but misunderstandings and alienation cast a dark shadow over the world of human and social relationships. Bitterness replaces affection: hatred comes in the place of love; and the ways of man towards men are strewn with thorns. Forster greatly cherishes the value of personal relations; they are for him the *sine qua non* of humanistic and liberal creed and, consequently, the blindness of the Anglo-Indians to them is the principal cause of the human and social tragedy he creates in this novel.

The political implications of *A Passage to India* have been emphasised and interpreted from various points of view. The view that the novel has been a powerful weapon in the hands of anti-imperialists has been emphasised by several critics and from different angles. Whereas liberal and academic critics praise *A Passage to India*, the imperialistically inclined Anglo-Indians and bureaucrats appeared to be annoyed by Forster's betrayal of the British cause in India. Forster has described, in *The Hill of Devi* (1953) a meeting between Sir Tukoji, the Maharajah of Dewas, and the Viceroy when adverse comments were made on *A Passage to India:*

> Another time he (H.H.) got some amusement out of *A Passage to India*. He dined at the Viceregal Lodge at Delhi soon after it had been published, and found that it was ill thought of there. Lady Reading did not care for it at all, and the newly appointed Indian member of Council expressed himself severely. (p.160)

The tragedy of the British Empire in India, Forster suggests, is in part due to the imposition on Indian tropical soil of the public school mentality of the British in India. Ronny Heaslop has no perception of the truth of personal relationships between the English and the Indian; the only bond he can conceive of is that which subsists between the ruler and the ruled. The failure of his private world, expressed in his inability to love Adela, is extended to his outer life; thus in Forster's own words the reader is made to realise that the life without reflects the life within. British public schools cultivated qualities of leadership, capacity for action, tact, courage and patriotism, but they also created narrowness and a feeling of superiority. They produced a blindness, Forster thought, to personal relations. The Anglo-Indian Club, the odd

Bridge Party, the dramatic trial scene and its ramifications contribute to the political image of the novel.

The discussion between Aziz and his friends about the English in India is very revealing and underlines the complex nature of Indo-British political and social relationships of that period. The English in England are good and hospitable, but on their arrival in British India they are claimed by the 'herd mentality' of the bureaucratic Anglo-India. They join the local tribe of Anglo-Indians and are thus drawn to the 'armies of the benighted.' Fielding is a singular exception and he is in many ways the representative of Forster's political point of view. His mind has been nourished on the values of culture and liberal education. He is close in spirit to that small but distinguished minority of English intellectuals who manned the civil service, some of whom made a great contribution to the renaissance of Indian arts and culture. Fielding is 'a holy man minus the holiness' and he swims against the main powerful current of Anglo-Indian community life in India.

The political image is marked by mutual distrust and fear between the Anglo-Indians and the Indians. Forster's portrayal of political and racial tensions in the wake of Aziz's trial and Mohurram and the spectacle of the panic of Anglo-Indians is considered by some critics to be rather exaggerated. The English in India can be accused of many failings but not of cowardice. Nonetheless, Forster's basic exposure of Anglo-India and the main implications of its portrayal seem valid.

Forster, however, does limit his portrayal of India, because he came into contact with Syed Ross Masood and Sir Tukoji, and the aristocracy of the princely states of Hyderabad and Dewas. By the force of circumstances during his stay in India, he remained outside the realm of resurgent British India. But this is not a serious limitation at all because the principal, dominant image that he projects in *A Passage to India* is neither social nor political, but essentially religious and spiritual. Social and racial elements are merely its outer forms, the inner substance is indeed a spiritual quest.

Religious and spiritual image

A Passage to India is basically a symbolical novel and its final meaning emerges out of a group of symbolic metaphors. The three sections of the novel make one organic, harmonious whole. While 'Mosque' symbolises the values of Islam, of unity and brotherhood of man, 'Caves' suggests primeval darkness and negation resulting in a breakdown of human relationships. 'Temple' signifies harmony and regeneration, the transformation of the wasteland into a green land, and a changeover from alienation to affection. The spiritual image in *A Passage to India* is presented through its three-fold symbolistic structure.

Forster's *A Passage to India* then, is a novel of cosmic significance. His men and women, even animals and apparently inanimate objects, such as rocks, participate in this cosmic drama. The situation Forster presents is dramatic and the whole world, the earth and the stars seem to participate in it. The first chapter, which is quite short, is itself a summary of the theme and symbolism of the whole novel:

> Except for the Marabar Caves—and they are twenty miles off—the city of Chandrapore presents nothing extraordinary. (p.5)

The extraordinary nature of the caves of hostile rock is suggested in the very first sentence and the chapter ends on a note of their aggressive quality: 'These fists and fingers are the Marabar Hills containing the extraordinary caves.' In the first chapter India and Anglo-India are physically divided: their descriptions faithfully convey the sense of separation. In the drama between Aziz and Fielding the caves and sky play their part and thus *A Passage to India* becomes a novel of cosmic significance. One of its principal themes is the concept of inclusion or exclusion from the Chain of Being and the world of salvation:

> In our Father's house are many mansions, they [Mr Graysfoot and young Mr Sorley] taught, and there alone will the incompatible multitudes of mankind be welcome and soothed. No one shall be turned away. . . . (pp.35–6)

Mr Sorley was inclined to admit monkeys and even jackals to this divine mansion but he 'became uneasy during the descent to wasps . . .' However, Mrs Moore, on observing a wasp seated on the tip of a peg, said, 'Pretty dear.'

The difference between the attitudes of the orthodox missionaries and Mrs Moore to the wasp is central to the meaning of this novel of cosmic significance. The thread of the wasp episode is picked up in the third section when Godbole, in an inspired mood, visualises the figure of the dead Mrs Moore with the wasp:

> . . . Chance brought her into his mind while it was in this heated state, he did not select her, she happened to occur among the throng of soliciting images, a tiny splinter, and he impelled her by his spiritual force to that place where completeness can be found. Completeness, not reconstruction. (p.288)

The wasp is beautiful but it has also a sting and therefore it becomes a symbol of good and evil. The missionaries could not admit it to their heaven but Mrs Moore, by virtue of her association with Godbole, accepts it and calls it 'Pretty dear.'

The theme of inclusion or exclusion is treated on another level. Whereas Godbole can accept the wasp, he becomes very uneasy about the stone. He dances on the carpet in a heated state and advances towards the stone but soon retreats to the carpet again since he is unable to include the stone. The stone episode is a clear reflection of Godbole's inability to be inclusive in this particular context, and provides another variation of the theme of inclusion and exclusion.

Godbole's moral cosmos is characterised by the coexistence of good and evil and is in accord with the Hindu view of God. The scene of Godbole's exposition of his philosophy and idea of God forms a significant link in the religious and spiritual pattern of the novel. Aziz is arrested on the charge of assault, Fielding is grieved and asks Godbole: 'Is Aziz innocent or guilty?' Godbole's answers, revealing both his own detachment and idea of the operative power of good and evil, baffle Fielding completely. And Fielding says to him, 'You're preaching that evil and good are the same.'

> 'Oh no, excuse me once again. Good and evil are different, as their names imply. But, in my own humble opinion, they are both of them aspects of my Lord. He is present in the one, absent in the other, and the difference between presence and absence is great, as great as my feeble mind can grasp. Yet absence implies presence, absence is not non-existence, and we are therefore entitled to repeat, "Come come, come, come." ' (p.179)

What is Godbole's view of God? He believes that God is one (a monistic view) and also that He is personal and has many incarnations (a theistic view) such as Siva, Vishnu and Krishna. These are different names of God, but He is essentially one. Godbole also believes in a personal God. His song shows that he is praising Tukaram, a Maharashtrian saint who lived in the seventeenth century. The followers of Vishnu, called Vaishnavas, are believers in a personal god. But Godbole goes further than the Vaishnavites and sings of a living, human, historical figure (Tukaram) as God. He sings: 'Tukaram, Thou art my father ... and my mother ... and everybody.' Forster's Godbole is obviously based on Sir Tukoji III, the Maharajah of Dewas, who, it is said, sang the same song in the novelist's presence at Dewas. Godbole's view of God therefore is wide and comprehensive enough to include His oneness as well as His incarnations, and even a real humanist saint as godhead.

East and West meet in harmony in the personality of Godbole, who is the truly prophetic character in *A Passage to India*; he provides an answer, at least partially, to the problem presented in the novel. The festival of Lord Krishna's birth symbolises renewal and regeneration, and Godbole's attempt to encompass everything, to transcend the chaos and nullity and to reach out to the unity and affirmation which lie beyond the transitory disorder, is a spiritual quest. His search for the spiritual is limited neither by place nor by time but is beyond them. He attempts to reach the absolute through a complete surrender of the self and extinction of his consciousness. And his valuation of life approximates to Forster's values, and therefore Godbole seems to be a prophetic character in *A Passage to India*. Even the redemptive power of Mrs Moore is partly derived from her spiritual link with Professor Godbole. To form the notion, however, that Hindus or Hindu mysticism provide the answer to the problem in *A Passage to India* would be to oversimplify its complexity.

What, then, is the image of India projected by Forster in *A Passage to India*? Forster's passage to India is indeed a 'Passage to More than India': it is surely the passage of man to the seas of God. The image of India is, of course, complex. Though the social, political and racial aspects of this image are important, the fundamental element is spiritual, and therefore the roles and implications of Mrs Moore and Godbole are central in the novel.

In *A Passage to India* Forster has found full expression because it is in this liberal classic that the aesthetic wholeness of his art is synthesised with his spiritual quest and visionary power. This is indeed the triumph of this novel which marks the apex of Forster's literary career.

Part 4

Hints for study

General suggestions

It is obvious that Forster's *A Passage to India* can be studied and understood on different levels. 'A truly great novel,' Middleton Murry stated, 'is a story to the simple, a parable for the wise or "a direct revelation of reality" to the man who has made it a part of his being.' Forster's *A Passage to India* may seem a tale to the simple, a parable to the judicious, and a dramatic exploration of reality at various levels to the more discriminating reader. The student is advised to choose simpler levels first and then to proceed slowly towards grasping the deeper layers of meaning.

The student is advised to study (*a*) the theme or themes, (*b*) the development of the narrative, (*c*) the major episodes (such as the visit to the Caves, the trial, etc.), (*d*) the role of the principal characters (Aziz, Fielding, Godbole, Mrs Moore, Adela, etc.), and (*e*) the structure of the novel or its three-fold division and its significance. He should try to grasp the various interpretations of Mrs Moore's and Adela's experiences in the Caves. Special attention needs to be given to the symbolic meanings of *A Passage to India* with particular reference to the Temple ceremonies. Forster's style or use of English for creative purposes should also be studied. The student must ask himself the basic question: What is *A Passage to India* about?

Suggested questions

In this short study various topics are dealt with, and relevant passages from the text are quoted with a view to showing the student ways of using quotations in support of his answers. Questions are suggested below which will test the student's knowledge of *A Passage to India* and his capacity to show that he has understood the novel and formed his own views about it.

1. Bring out the significance of the principal themes of *A Passage to India*.
2. Explain and illustrate the significance of the title of *A Passage to India*.

3. Write a critical note on the structure of *A Passage to India*.
4. Examine the symbolic significance of the three-fold division of the novel, 'Mosque,' 'Caves,' and 'Temple'.
5. The first chapter of *A Passage to India*, though short, is crucial to its understanding. Examine this view.
6. Examine *A Passage to India* as a political novel or a novel of race relations.
7. *A Passage to India* is essentially the creation of Forster's 'liberal imagination'.
8. 'The Bridge Party is a masterstroke of Forster's irony and humour.' Discuss this statement.
9. Examine the implications of the meeting of Aziz and Mrs Moore in the mosque and its effect on later events in *A Passage to India*.
10. Compare the Bridge Party and Fielding's tea, showing how differently Forster describes the two episodes.
11. Examine the symbolic significance of Godbole's Song at Fielding's party.
12. The role of the Marabar Caves in *A Passage to India* is in part a mystery and in part a muddle. Critically examine this episode in the novel.
13. Attempt your own interpretation of what actually happened in the Marabar Caves.
14. Write a critical note on Mrs Moore's experience in the Caves.
15. What are the probable causes of Adela's strange experience or hallucination in the Caves?
16. Did Mrs Moore experience 'vision' or 'nightmare', 'anti-vision' or 'double vision' in the Caves? Give reasons for your answer.
17. Narrate the events of Aziz's trial leading to mass hysteria and Adela's recantation.
18. Describe in your own words Godbole's participation in the celebration of the Lord's birth.
19. Examine the impact of the *bhakti* cult or 'universal love' on the characters and situation in the third section of *A Passage to India*.
20. Elaborate the symbolic significance of the 'Temple' ceremonies in *A Passage to India*.
21. Write a character sketch of Aziz.
22. Is Godbole a shadowy and insubstantial character? Discuss.
23. Discuss the part played by Fielding in *A Passage to India*.
24. Write a critical note, giving examples, on the style of *A Passage to India*.
25. Examine and illustrate the main characteristics of Forster's style and technique in *A Passage to India*.

Some questions and suggested answers

---

1. Discuss the character and personality of Fielding

Cyril Fielding was essentially a cultured humanist, an ardent educator, an agnostic and a warm-hearted man. He was a sweet-tempered, hard-bitten, intelligent man in his forties, with a strong belief in the efficacy of education and culture. He was Principal of the Chandrapore College and enjoyed teaching all levels of pupils.

His role as a liberal educationist brought him closer to Indians and at the same time alienated him from official segments of Anglo-India. He was patriotic and friendly in England but in India he found himself divided from local British officialdom primarily because of his liberal creed. The local Anglo-Indians disliked and distrusted him because he was a disruptive force in their official ranks. He disbelieved in their herd-instinct, because his mind was nourished on values of personal relations and individual integrity. He was also a conscientious educator and a man of ideas. Since 'ideas are fatal to caste', he was not much appreciated by Anglo-India, especially by its women. Fielding believed in the holiness of the heart's affections:

> The world, he believed, is a globe of men who are trying to reach one another and can best do so by the help of good will plus culture and intelligence—a creed ill suited to Chandrapore, but he had come out too late to lose it. He had no racial feeling—not because he was superior to his brother civilians, but because he had matured in a different atmosphere, where the herd-instinct does not flourish (p.60).

Fielding was not an Anglo-Indian 'sahib', and though the Anglo-Indian women disliked him, he was not interested in them at all. He began to like and love the company of Indians. In this aspect Fielding seems to represent Forster.

Fielding was untidy and very informal in his behaviour. He possessed a fund of goodwill and geniality. He went to Aziz's house to enquire about his health, a generous gesture which was deeply appreciated. He told his Muslim friends that he did not believe in God. His professed atheism or indifference to belief or disbelief shocked them, and in consequence, they asked him ... 'if this is the case, how is England justified in holding India?' Whereas the Indians claimed to be 'spiritual', Fielding said he was a 'holy man minus the holiness.'

He was excessively kind in his behaviour towards his Indian friends, but was sometimes puzzled whether it required 'an occasional intoxication of the blood' (p.115). He was friendly, but not quite intimate with Aziz, or for that matter, with anyone. He was not well disposed towards marriage because he would 'far rather leave a thought behind him than a child' (p.117). Whereas Aziz was to a degree sex-conscious (he talks of ladies 'with breasts like mangoes', p.118), Fielding was rather unresponsive to women's charms and the idea of marriage. He also believed in steadfast adherence to personal values. If differences occurred, he said, he was willing to leave as he was used to travelling light. His fundamental belief lay in individualism, in 'teaching people to be individuals and to understand other individuals.'

His credo, or set of beliefs, is derived from European or Western liberalism, from his favourite 'Mediterranean norm'. It is to this norm, this code of conduct, this set of beliefs that he finally returns. Aziz and Fielding meet and become close friends, and then misunderstandings develop. These are partly cleared, friendship is restored to a degree and they go for 'their last ride' in the Mau jungles. In this last scene they part company, when neither the horse, nor the earth, nor the sky wants their friendship to continue: 'No, not yet,' and the sky said, 'No, not there.' Whether this is a defeatist ending and a frustrating finale to the saga of their friendship is indeed an open question. If *A Passage to India* is considered merely a story of their mutual friendship, the end is surely discouraging, if not altogether defeatist. It is on this rather ambivalent note that the narrative of *A Passage to India* ends.

The boating scene in 'Temple' in which the boats collide symbolises the reassurance of friendship, the clearing of the clouds of distrust between Aziz and Fielding. Aziz even went so far as to write a letter to Adela ... but the impact of the unity and love is transitory. The old divisions seem to return to the world of *A Passage to India*.

It is in this context that Fielding's return to England, to the Mediterranean 'norm', to the joys of 'form' in Venice has to be understood. Does this return constitute a withdrawal of his liberal creed? The answer is surely 'no' because the Mediterranean is also the human norm. Fielding seeks harmony between 'the works of man and the earth that upholds them' (p.283), and therefore his journey back home is part of his continual quest for a civilisation free from muddle.

2. Write on the character and personality of Professor Godbole

Professor Narayan Godbole is an enigmatic character, and has given rise to varied and conflicting interpretations. He is not a 'flat' character as many readers are likely to assume, but a 'round' one, who undergoes changes in the process of becoming. In fact some readers believe, though perhaps erroneously, that there are two Godboles instead of one in *A*

Passage to India. One is the somewhat insubstantial and ambiguous figure in 'Mosque' and 'Caves', and the other a powerful, potent, benign influence in the 'Temple' section, who becomes almost the embodiment of the Forsterian Voice. The Godbole whom we meet at Fielding's tea party is a quiet Brahmin from the Deccan, the southern part of India, who speaks very little, and perhaps conceals more than he reveals. He is an embodiment of harmony, a synthesis of East and West, a genuine and true friend. In 'Mosque' and 'Caves' he seems to be some sort of philosopher; he talks about the Hindu view of God, of good and evil and a godly or godless universe. His comment on what happened to Aziz in the Caves baffles Fielding. He had miscalculated the length of a prayer which had resulted in their missing the train to the Marabar Caves. At Fielding's tea party, Godbole sings a song of invocation to Lord Krishna, 'Come, come, come'. But 'he refuses' to come. In contrast to this social world, Godbole (in the third section 'Temple') is shown dancing on a strip of red carpet in the presence of God. From the cry 'Come, come' and the 'refusal to come', this is indeed a soul's long journey into a different world.

However, Godbole, too, is an embodiment of friendship which has to be realised through love. He helps Aziz to get settled in Mau and is full of compassion and affection for him. The question whether he has been indifferent to Aziz earlier in his moment of disaster and misfortune is challenging. The answer to this question has to be found in religious values, since Godbole's love operates in a world which is totally different from Fielding's. Whereas the Christian world demands an immediate sympathy for the suffering individual, the Hindu cosmos emphasises the universality of love with a large sense of all-inclusiveness of being, and without any specific concentration on the individual. Godbole is also influenced by the Hindu sense of detachment, which modifies his instinctive and immediate responses to Aziz. However, he is inwardly involved in Aziz's welfare, and, in fact, becomes an instrument in cementing the bonds of friendship between Aziz and Fielding in the third section of the novel.

Godbole, in his conversation with Fielding about Aziz's disaster, speaks about 'good and evil' as 'two aspects of my Lord.' He says:

'Good and evil are different, as their names imply. But in my own humble opinion, they are both of them aspects of my Lord. He is present in the one, absent in the other, and the difference between presence and absence is great, as great as my feeble mind can grasp. Yet absence implies presence, absence is not non-existence, and we are therefore entitled to repeat, "Come, come, come, come." ' (p.179)

This view of God highlights His all-inclusiveness and also the monistic interpretation of reality. Monism, from the Greek for single, is a philosophical idea which holds that there is but one fundamental reality in the universe. Although the view that good and evil are both aspects of the divine emphasises the monistic view, the second statement that 'God is present in the one, absent in the other', and the difference between 'absence and presence' is great, modifies the above-mentioned position.

This interpretation is valuable because it paves the way for Godbole's major role in the ceremonies of Lord Krishna's birth; he seems to hold the view that there is one God who is personal, the Creator of the world, and the ground of all existence. Do the utterances and actions of Godbole signify this movement from one single reality to a personal god in his religious beliefs? This is another complex question which has to be answered with a view to interpreting the full significance of Godbole's role and personality in the novel.

The answer to this question is partly, 'Yes'. Godbole surely moves to a theistic view of the universe (that there is one God who is personal) and because he sings of Tukaram, the great Maharashtrian saint belonging to the principal Hindu belief of the Vaishnava cult. The followers of Vishnu are ardent believers in a personal god. It is precisely this philosophical or religious context which becomes the principal religious element in 'Temple', the third section of *A Passage to India*. Godbole's hymn 'Tukaram, thou art my father ... and my mother' is sung not in praise of Krishna, the Hindu god, but in praise of the great saint-poet who was a remarkable devotee of Krishna or Vishnu. In effect, Krishna (or Rama) is another name of Vishnu, the Hindu god. Krishna is an *avatar* (meaning incarnation) of Vishnu and is indeed a redemptive god, who seems to dominate Forster's world-view in 'Temple'.

What Mrs Moore hears in the Caves is an echo, which is a reaction to the sound inside. This sound is sometimes explained as 'Oum' or 'Oam', which is the sacred syllable of the Hindu religion. This Marabar sound or echo is sometimes linked with a religious experience.

---

3. Write brief notes on some of the minor characters in *A Passage to India*

Ronny Heaslop is a British public school product who has gone out to India with a well-developed body and mind, but an underdeveloped heart. His failure is rooted in his incapacity to create and develop personal relations. He is a young 'sahib', imperial in attitude and even imperious in behaviour. He ruins Fielding's tea party by his odd conduct towards the Indians. While he is rather 'petty' towards Indians, he is indeed decent in his behaviour towards his own countrymen. 'My temper's rotten, I must apologise' (p.81), he admits to Adela. When she announces that they 'are not going to be married,' he takes it quietly, though the decision hurts him greatly. The fact that Adela and Ronny do not quarrel over their decision is a measure of their common sense, cool-headedness and rationality. This, says Forster, is typically 'British'. Adela remarks 'We've been awfully British over it, but I suppose that's all right.' 'As we are British, I suppose it is,' answers Ronny (p.83).

Although Ronny is sometimes tactless and, as is expected of sahibs, makes rows over small matters (for example, over the servant's delay), he is quite conscious of his duties in administering a difficult country and keeping the peace (the typical argument for imperialism). He has many redeeming qualities. His sense of duty, loyalty to Anglo-India, sense of fair play, and his behaviour towards Adela, subsequent to the trial, show him as a typical British middle-class civil servant intent on doing his duty in a difficult situation.

Major Callendar is somewhat an arrogant person whose portrait is marked by the dark hues of British imperialism in India. He is very rude to Aziz. He sends for him at his house and does not even leave a message. The servant is too polite to repeat his words 'Damn Aziz ...' Callendar is not as skilful a surgeon as Aziz, and this makes him even more overbearing. His treatment of Nureddin is almost inhuman and ghastly. He is reported to have said, 'I have tortured that nigger. ...' (p.236). He is said to have put pepper instead of antiseptic on Nureddin's wounds. The victory procession is to march toward Minto Hospital to maltreat Major Callendar, but the situation is saved and disaster averted by Dr Panna Lal. Dr Lal says that he has only told lies to Aziz, and that the story of ill-treatment is false. Whether this story is true or false, the fact remains that the Major is aggressive in his attitudes and actions towards Indians. He is said to have employed Dr Panna Lal as a spy to find whether Aziz is really ill or is merely shamming. The Major and Mrs Callendar are indeed most detestable characters.

Mr Turton, the Collector of Chandrapore, is almost a caricature. He arranged a party, the Bridge Party, which was a failure, though he played his part well as a host. Mr Turton was highly enraged over the alleged assault on Adela in the Caves. He watched Aziz's arrest from inside the waiting room. Mr Turton paid no attention to Fielding's protests. He was deeply shaken by this catastrophe. He has been in Chandrapore for about six years and lamented that all the reputation of the district was lost in the dust. He is sometimes involved in his own emotions and then he breaks down. He believes in courtesy and quiet official relationships with the Indians. He is therefore opposed to Fielding and to his faith in personal relations, which seem to him disastrous 'modern ideas'. However, he, too, has redeeming features. He is a believer in fair play and justice, and he prevents Aziz's luggage from being stolen on the platform. He also keeps a cool head in a trying situation. However, when provoked bitterly, Turton's reactions are rather hostile. He would say to the Indians: 'You shall pay for this. You shall squeal' (p.166). Turton finally becomes a figure of fun and degenerates into a caricature though Forster shows the rudiments of fair play and decency in his character.

4. Write on the final meaning of *A Passage to India*: expansion and not completion

The question of the final meaning of *A Passage to India* is a complex aspect of the novel. There are moments of vision and anti-vision in it, for instance, the Krishna festival and the 'boum' of the Caves. Neither the moments of despair or defeat nor the moments of hope or victory lead to a distinct understanding of a lasting wholeness.

Every attempt at a synthesis is followed by a new antithesis, for something is always left unaccounted for—the wasp by the missionaries and the stone by Godbole—and the circle has to be endlessly extended. Such a view demonstrates Forster's own theory that his novel aimed not at completion but at expansion.

Part 5

Suggestions for further reading

The text

The uniform edition of *A Passage to India*, Edward Arnold, London, 1971 is cited in these notes. The novel was first published by Edward Arnold, London, 1924, and Harcourt Brace, New York, 1924. It is available in the Penguin Modern Classics Series, Penguin Books, Harmondsworth, 1961.

General reading

BEER, J.B.: *The Achievement of E.M. Forster*. Chatto and Windus, London, 1962. A sensitive reading of *A Passage to India*.

BRADBURY, MALCOLM (ED.): *Forster: A Collection of Critical Essays*. Prentice-Hall, Englewood Cliffs, N.J. 1966. A collection of essays representing both American and British points of view.

COLMER, JOHN.: *E.M. Forster: A Passage to India*. Edward Arnold, London, 1967. A very short study of *A Passage to India*

GRANSDEN, K.W.: *E.M. Forster*. Oliver and Boyd, Edinburgh and London, 1962. Observes Forster's *A Passage to India* as his 'final corrective to liberal humanism'.

KIRKPATRICK, B.J.: *A Bibliography of E.M. Forster*. Rupert Hart-Davis, London, 1965. Very useful for students wishing to continue their study of E.M. Forster.

LEVINE, JUNE PERRY: *Creation and Criticism: A Passage to India*. Chatto and Windus, London, 1971. This considers the historical background of *A Passage to India*, the 'raw material' and the 'text' of the novel.

MCCONKEY, JAMES: *The Novels of E.M. Forster*. Cornell University Press, Ithaca, 1957. A perceptive reading of *A Passage to India* from the viewpoints of 'rhythm' and 'prophecy.'

SHAHANE, V.A.: *E.M. Forster: A Study in Double Vision*. Arnold-Heinemann, New Delhi, 1975. This assesses *A Passage to India* as an expression of Forster's 'Double Vision.'

SHAHANE, V.A. (ED.): *Perspectives on E.M. Forster's A Passage to India: A Collection of Critical Essays.* Barnes and Noble, New York, 1968. A collection of critical, mostly American, essays.

SHAHANE, V.A. (ED.): *Focus on Forster's A Passage to India: Indian Essays in Criticism.* Orient Longman, Madras, 1972. Indian interpretations of the novel published to mark the fiftieth anniversary of its publication (in 1974).

SHAHANE, V.A. (ED.): *Approaches to E.M. Forster.* Arnold-Heinemann, New Delhi, 1981. Papers presented at the International Seminar and Celebrations of Forster's Birth Centenary held at Hyderabad in January 1979.

STALLYBRASS, OLIVER (ED.): *Aspects of E.M. Forster.* Edward Arnold, London, 1969. Biographical and critical essays, useful for further study of E.M. Forster.

STONE, WILFRED: *The Cave and the Mountain:* A Study of E.M. Forster. Stanford University Press, Stanford, 1966; Oxford University Press, London, 1966. This provides exhaustive and detailed readings of the novels.

THOMSON, GEORGE H: *The Fiction of E.M. Forster.* Wayne State University Press, Detroit, 1967. One of the best criticisms of *A Passage to India* in its symbolical and archetypal contexts.

TRILLING, LIONEL: *E.M. Forster.* The Hogarth Press, London, 1944. Incisive early study of E.M. Forster as liberal humanist and artist.

The author of these notes

VASANT A. SHAHANE was educated at Fergusson College, Bombay University and the University of Leeds. His publications include *E.M. Forster, A. Reassessment* (1962), *Perspectives on A Passage to India* (1968), *Notes on Walt Whitman's Leaves of Grass* (1972), *Rudyard Kipling. Activist and Artist* (1973), *Khushwant Singh* (1972), *Focus on A Passage to India* (1975), *Forster. A Study in Double Vision* (1975), *Ruth Prawer Jhabvala* (1976). He has served as a Visiting Professor at Wisconsin University and at Wayne State University. He is a Senior Professor and Chairman, Department of English, Osmania University, Hydarabad.

York Notes: list of titles

CHINUA ACHEBE
Things Fall Apart

EDWARD ALBEE
Who's Afraid of Virginia Woolf?

MARGARET ATWOOD
The Handmaid's Tale

W. H. AUDEN
Selected Poems

JANE AUSTEN
Emma
Mansfield Park
Northanger Abbey
Persuasion
Pride and Prejudice
Sense and Sensibility

SAMUEL BECKETT
Waiting for Godot

ARNOLD BENNETT
The Card

JOHN BETJEMAN
Selected Poems

WILLIAM BLAKE
Songs of Innocence, Songs of Experience

ROBERT BOLT
A Man For All Seasons

CHARLOTTE BRONTË
Jane Eyre

EMILY BRONTË
Wuthering Heights

ROBERT BURNS
Selected Poems

BYRON
Selected Poems

GEOFFREY CHAUCER
The Franklin's Tale
The Knight's Tale
The Merchant's Tale
The Miller's Tale
The Nun's Priest's Tale
The Pardoner's Tale
Prologue to the Canterbury Tales
The Wife of Bath's Tale

SAMUEL TAYLOR COLERIDGE
Selected Poems

JOSEPH CONRAD
Heart of Darkness

DANIEL DEFOE
Moll Flanders
Robinson Crusoe

SHELAGH DELANEY
A Taste of Honey

CHARLES DICKENS
Bleak House
David Copperfield
Great Expectations
Hard Times
Oliver Twist

EMILY DICKINSON
Selected Poems

JOHN DONNE
Selected Poems

DOUGLAS DUNN
Selected Poems

GERALD DURRELL
My Family and Other Animals

GEORGE ELIOT
Middlemarch
The Mill on the Floss
Silas Marner

T. S. ELIOT
Four Quartets
Murder in the Cathedral
Selected Poems
The Waste Land

HENRY FIELDING
Joseph Andrews
Tom Jones

F. SCOTT FITZGERALD
The Great Gatsby
Tender is the Night

GUSTAVE FLAUBERT
Madame Bovary

E. M. FORSTER
Howards End
A Passage to India

JOHN FOWLES
The French Lieutenant's Woman

ELIZABETH GASKELL
North and South

WILLIAM GOLDING
Lord of the Flies

OLIVER GOLDSMITH
She Stoops to Conquer

GRAHAM GREENE
Brighton Rock
The Heart of the Matter
The Power and the Glory

THOMAS HARDY
Far from the Madding Crowd

Jude the Obscure
The Mayor of Casterbridge
The Return of the Native
Selected Poems
Tess of the D'Urbervilles

L. P. HARTLEY
The Go-Between

NATHANIEL HAWTHORNE
The Scarlet Letter

SEAMUS HEANEY
Selected Poems

ERNEST HEMINGWAY
A Farewell to Arms
The Old Man and the Sea

SUSAN HILL
I'm the King of the Castle

HOMER
The Iliad
The Odyssey

GERARD MANLEY HOPKINS
Selected Poems

TED HUGHES
Selected Poems

ALDOUS HUXLEY
Brave New World

HENRY JAMES
The Portrait of a Lady

BEN JONSON
The Alchemist
Volpone

JAMES JOYCE
Dubliners
A Portrait of the Artist as a Young Man

JOHN KEATS
Selected Poems

PHILIP LARKIN
Selected Poems

D. H. LAWRENCE
The Rainbow
Selected Short Stories
Sons and Lovers
Women in Love

HARPER LEE
To Kill a Mockingbird

LAURIE LEE
Cider with Rosie

CHRISTOPHER MARLOWE
Doctor Faustus

ARTHUR MILLER
The Crucible
Death of a Salesman
A View from the Bridge

JOHN MILTON
Paradise Lost I & II
Paradise Lost IV & IX

SEAN O'CASEY
Juno and the Paycock

GEORGE ORWELL
Animal Farm
Nineteen Eighty-four

JOHN OSBORNE
Look Back in Anger

WILFRED OWEN
Selected Poems

HAROLD PINTER
The Caretaker

SYLVIA PLATH
Selected Works

ALEXANDER POPE
Selected Poems

J. B. PRIESTLEY
An Inspector Calls

JEAN RHYS
The Wide Sargasso Sea

J. D. SALINGER
The Catcher in the Rye

WILLIAM SHAKESPEARE
Antony and Cleopatra
As You Like It
Coriolanus
Hamlet
Henry IV Part I
Henry IV Part II
Henry V
Julius Caesar
King Lear
Macbeth
Measure for Measure
The Merchant of Venice
A Midsummer Night's Dream
Much Ado About Nothing
Othello
Richard II
Richard III
Romeo and Juliet
Sonnets
The Taming of the Shrew
The Tempest
Twelfth Night
The Winter's Tale

GEORGE BERNARD SHAW
Arms and the Man
Pygmalion
Saint Joan

MARY SHELLEY
Frankenstein

PERCY BYSSHE SHELLEY
Selected Poems

RICHARD BRINSLEY SHERIDAN
The Rivals

R. C. SHERRIFF
Journey's End

MURIEL SPARK
The Prime of Miss Jean Brodie

JOHN STEINBECK
The Grapes of Wrath
Of Mice and Men
The Pearl

TOM STOPPARD
Rosencrantz and Guildenstern are Dead

JONATHAN SWIFT
Gulliver's Travels

JOHN MILLINGTON SYNGE
The Playboy of the Western World

MILDRED D. TAYLOR
Roll of Thunder, Hear My Cry

W. M. THACKERAY
Vanity Fair

MARK TWAIN
Huckleberry Finn

VIRGIL
The Aeneid

DEREK WALCOTT
Selected Poems

ALICE WALKER
The Color Purple

JOHN WEBSTER
The Duchess of Malfi

OSCAR WILDE
The Importance of Being Earnest

TENNESSEE WILLIAMS
Cat on a Hot Tin Roof
A Streetcar Named Desire

VIRGINIA WOOLF
Mrs Dalloway
To the Lighthouse

WILLIAM WORDSWORTH
Selected Poems

W. B. YEATS
Selected Poems